A Cup of Comfort

for Courage

Stories that celebrate everyday
heroism, strength, and triumph

EDITED BY
COLLEEN SELL

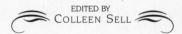

ADAMS MEDIA
Avon, Massachusetts

For my son, Mickey—my hero.

Published by
Adams Media, an F+W Publications Company
57 Littlefield Street, Avon, MA 02322. U.S.A.
www.adamsmedia.com and *www.cupofcomfort.com*

ISBN: 1-59337-003-2

Printed in Canada.
J I H G F E D C B A

Library of Congress Cataloging-in-Publication Data
available from publisher

Cover illustration by Eulala Conner.

This book is available at quantity discounts for bulk purchases.
For information, call 1-800-872-5627.

Acknowledgments

It takes courage to write, even more so to write honestly and compellingly about powerful personal experiences. And so I stand in awe and appreciation of the authors whose stories grace these pages.

My sincere thanks go to the outstanding team at Adams Media for their vision and support—with a special tip of the hat to Kate Epstein, for her steady command and comic relief.

I am most grateful to the heroes in my life who encourage and enable me to do the work I love: my fiercely supportive parents, siblings, children, and grandchildren; my mentor and pal, Richard Krevolin; my dearest friend, Judy Sebille; and my devoted husband, T.N. Trudeau.

Contents

Introduction

"Conscience is the root of all true courage."

—James Freeman Clarke

Many years ago, in my ninth grade social studies class, my classmates and I were given an assignment to write an essay entitled, "What Is Courage?" The next day, a few of the essays were read out loud in class, and then we debated the meaning of courage. Even the teacher was surprised at the many different definitions and examples of courage that we discussed. The one thing we all agreed upon was that courage comes from within— that it is conscience giving rise to positive action.

Since then, I've learned much more about courage from many people whose brave deeds and heroic lives have provided innumerable lessons on the depth and breadth of courage. Some I've been privileged to know—like my grandfather, Frank Baum, a highly decorated veteran of three wars who went on to fight, and win, his own personal war with post-traumatic-stress-related alcoholism. I've never met many of the heroes who've influenced and inspired my life. Only a few are celebrated icons, like Katharine Hepburn, Jimmy Carter, and Martin Luther King Jr. Most are unsung, everyday heroes—like the child from the ghetto who rises above it; the brokenhearted widow who dares to love again; the senior who braves the wild, wild Internet; and the firefighter who rescues a family from their burning home.

But my greatest lessons in courage began in 1994, more than three decades after my introduction to courage in my ninth grade social studies class. This time my teacher was my then eighteen-year-old son, Mickey. Nine years later, he continues to teach me the true meaning of courage, in all its manifestations, every day.

Shortly after graduating from high school and just days before he was to begin his freshman year of college, Mickey sustained a serious brain injury that nearly killed him and that ended his life as he'd known it and the life he'd planned. Although his intellect remained intact, he lost virtually everything else—his mental and physical health, his friends, his independence, his dignity, his hopes, his dreams—all trapped in a cacophony of confusion, depression, anxiety, and, at times, psychosis. He could no longer work or go to school, play basketball or his guitar, drive a car or hold a conversation, read, watch television, or even hug. Over the course of six years, he spent a total of thirty-four months, nearly three years, in hospitals and residential rehabilitation facilities, growing increasingly sicker and more isolated, subjected to the rejection, poverty, and humiliating treatment so often experienced by people with severe neurobiological disorders.

And yet, he persevered. He never gave in or gave up. He tried unceasingly to find his way back, to focus his tormented mind, to understand his illness, to be self-reliant, to be useful, to be kind. He tried treatment after treatment, even though none were effective, many made him worse, and most caused horrific side effects. And after five years of steady decline with no relief, when he felt that he could try no more and wanted only to be released from his living hell, he hung in there and agreed to try one last, very risky course of treatment.

Within days of starting the new medication, Mickey started to improve. Two weeks later, he smiled, hugged me, and played his beloved guitar for the first time in years. Three months later he was released from the hospital and began the daunting task of rebuilding his life. One of the first things he did was to enroll in his first college class. He aced it. Three years later, he continues to attend college part-time, to live independently, and to make steady progress toward his goals.

Mickey's journey to recovery isn't over and it still isn't easy; it probably never will be. He says that's okay, that he's just grateful for the opportunity to one day live a productive and meaningful life, to maybe have a family someday, to "be a good person." He says that he's lucky. I say he's courageous.

In this special collection, we share the amazing stories of several extraordinary, ordinary heroes. I hope they will inspire you—just as my son, Mickey Hansen Jr., has inspired me—to let your conscience be your comfort, your guide, and your strength.

—*Colleen Sell*

Something More

The Australian summer sun beats on the thirsty bush. It burns my legs through the windscreen as I rattle over deeply corrugated dirt roads. It is mid-January in the central highlands of Tasmania, and I am here alone, recently single, recently in my thirties, and in need of physical and spiritual challenge. Over the next four weeks I will go into some of the remotest areas of the state, to walk and camp in the wilderness. In a few days I will join a handful of others on an eleven-day rafting trip down 125 kilometers (approximately 80 miles) of the Franklin River, in the inaccessible wilderness of Tasmania's southwest. But right now, this adventurer fears she may be lost. I long for the sight of a paved road.

As I drive, my thoughts collide with one another and I am uncomfortably alone with them. The last year has been hell, and I am raw from many losses.

I am a pilgrim here, searching for physical hardship, for risk to plunge into. I want hard mountains, drenching rain, and big, frightening rapids to shock away my numbness. I am here to feel alive again.

After many long, hot hours, I reach the west coast. Painted with dust and melting under the late afternoon sun, I pull into the tiny coastal town of Strahan, never before so happy to see cars and buildings. Some frontier woman I am.

I check into my hostel, kick open the door to my bunkroom, and blink in the darkness of the musty room.

Then I see her. Smiling, staring directly at me as though I am expected, she is perched like a doll on the edge of a sagging bunk bed. The sight of her face stops me at the threshold for a few moments. I am very surprised to see this stranger. She is terribly old. Her tiny, frail form reminds me of my late mother. Her smile is a bit unsettling.

"My name is Vonny Helberg," she says. "But you can call me Gran Vonny. Everyone does."

Beside her on the bed lies a fractured range of odds and ends, spilling from a well-traveled vinyl suitcase. Tiny crocheted flowers, shreds of notes and papers, tubes of antiseptic cream, bandages.

"Hello," I say.

Polite conversation ensues as I search for swimming gear, uncomfortable in the presence of my unlikely roommate. I feel an overwhelming responsibility to take care of her. *What on earth is this tiny old woman doing here in a youth hostel?*

I find my gear, smile a goodbye, and head out to explore. But I cannot shake the image of that expectant smile.

When I return later that night, she is asleep. I creep up to my bunk and ease my exhausted body into the sleeping bag, fading into sweet oblivion.

Sometime later, I am disturbed by the entry of two female backpackers. Perfumed with excesses of the local brew, they fall spectacularly over chairs and packs, swearing in German while trying to insert themselves in bed. Gran Vonny stirs. I feel anxious. *Shut up*, I think. *Don't you know there's an elderly woman in here trying to get some sleep?*

This is absurd. Damn it. This was supposed to be a girl's own adventure. Instead, I am in a room with an old woman I feel responsible for. I don't even know her! It's all too close to the home I'm here to escape from.

I fall asleep, dreaming dreams of my mother in her final weeks, pale and aged in her hospital bed.

When I awake, the only sign of the old lady is her neat bags on the bunk. The German girls snore softly, faces crammed into pillows beneath tangled, sun-streaked locks. Their slumbering exhalation of last night's beer drives me out of the dorm and into the communal kitchen. Gran Vonny is there, writing in a small book. We smile our good mornings.

"Are you a writer?" I ask, not expecting her to be at all, but wanting to make conversation.

"Oh, yes. I'm writing about Sarah Island."

Sarah Island—one of the most brutal penal settlements in Tasmanian history, jutting from the wild waters of Macquarie Harbour, near Strahan. Convicts died in droves there, from brutal punishments, disease, and exposure. Now it's a historic site, the cells little more than crumbling ruins.

"I've always wanted to write about it, about those poor convicts. I even spent the night there a few years ago." She sips hot tea. "In a tree, as a matter of fact."

My face must be registering the thought that perhaps this lady is a bit mad. Her serene smile now suggests mischief.

"The tide came in. I went over there for a week, so I could experience a little of what they did, to help the writing. I didn't take much with me. It rained terribly hard. Then a big flood tide came, so I climbed a tree for the night."

"When was this?"

"Oh . . . let's see . . . hmm, about ten years ago."

Oh, my God. She was in her seventies. . . .

"Do you write?" She fixes me with bright eyes.

"Ah. No. Well, I do but I . . . I'm not a writer," I stumble, feeling as though I've been caught out somehow.

She's still smiling.

"I've always wanted to be a writer." I blurt it out, like a child's confession.

"Well. You probably already are one." And still she smiles.

It is clearly time to shift the heat. I begin to ask her about herself, and a remarkable tale unfolds.

Vonny has just returned from Indonesia, where she works voluntarily in the slums, treating orphans' scratches and sores with her tubes of antiseptic cream and bandages. It's not much, she says, but the children have nothing at all. There is no support for this venture. She does it all herself, living frugally and spending everything she has to finance her mission. She has no home, no possessions. I am gobsmacked. Clearly Gran Vonny is not the frail old lady I had taken her for on first sight.

"What about family? Do you have anyone here in Tasmania?" I ask.

"No, no one. I was engaged once, many years ago. But he was killed in the war, and when you've truly loved, you don't see the point in going for anything less after that. There's been no one else."

All of this has been said so simply, as though the decision to be alone for her whole life was as simple as choosing a brand of soap. My own recently broken heart, which had reduced me to near ashes, now seems trivial when I consider what Vonny has been through. She is so alone, yet she claims not to be lonely—she has her Indonesian children. *How can anyone be this generous?*

I finish my breakfast and excuse myself, explaining that I am taking a flight over the Franklin River this morning, to see it from the air before I begin my rafting trip.

"You'll see Sarah then," says Vonny, looking wistful. "I would love to see it—and the Franklin." Her face animates. "I protested that dam you know, back in 1983."

I remembered the campaign. The Tasmanian government had planned to build a dam that would have flooded the entire valley, destroying one of the world's greatest rivers. It was a fierce fight, with "greenies" on one side, camping in the wet forests for weeks on end, enduring assaults and arrest, and the furious hydro workers on the other, enraged at the prospect of losing their jobs should the dam be stopped.

The conservation movement won, and the Franklin Dam was never built. The river was declared a World Heritage Wilderness Area, forever protected. And Vonny was part of its preservation.

As I drive to catch my flight, I imagine her among the bedraggled greenies in the forest, chatting and drinking hot tea in the rain, affixing bandages to bruised protesters. And resisting arrest. *How many more surprises does this woman have for me?*

Soon, I am soaring above the river, looking with growing excitement at the site of my impending adventure. But I am also thinking of Vonny: Giving her life to begging children in the streets of Indonesia. Writing her stories and sleeping in trees and rainforest. Devoting her life to something real. I realize that I'm here on a joyride. A week ago I had been boasting to my friends about the dangerous adventure I was about to undertake, lapping up their admiration at my courage. In reality, I am buying my adventure, paying other people to take me through it safely and making sure I get my money's worth. It is beginning to feel hollow.

I have lived completely for myself, and still I want more. More fulfillment, more experiences, more recognition, more love. Selfless acts are a rare thing in my life. I have plenty of opinions about what is right, but I have never taken those values any further than heated discussions at dinner parties.

When I first saw Vonny I felt sorry for her—a lonely old lady with nothing in her life, I'd thought. But now I admired her and felt humbled. There was no need to pity Gran Vonny.

When we land, I walk toward my car, the hollowness not quite faded. Then, on impulse, I turn and quickly go back to the wharf.

The next day Vonny and I exchange addresses. Time to drive to Hobart and meet up with my group for the Franklin trip. I hug her gently, her tiny bones feeling like bird wings in my embrace. Before I leave, I press an envelope into her hand. "Something you need to do," I say.

As I drive, I wonder what this big adventure of mine is really all about. I feel changed by the past two days, challenged. Certainly, I no longer feel like the strong, brave woman I had assumed myself to be. Not like her.

Weeks later, in my apartment in the city, I open my first letter from her. She tells me all about the flight I had surprised her with, how she had seen all the beauty and history she had loved and fought for. She saw yellow rafts far below and wondered if I was in one. I was. She congratulates me for my adventuresome spirit. But for all the rapids in that beautiful river, I never really had to be brave. I did learn something about courage in Tasmania, but from a tiny woman in her eighties, over cups of hot tea in the kitchen of a youth hostel.

That trip was years ago now. I've since moved to Tasmania. For a while, I worked in the wilderness, guiding bushwalks. I fell in love with the place and found my own beloved. I think I understand a little of what Vonny meant about true love now. Yet, in my life, I still strive to discover my own real courage. I'm still challenged to make the choice to really live for something beyond myself. I'd like to think that I am closer than I was before. I'd like to think that the strength of spirit I witnessed in that tiny, extraordinary woman will inspire me to live in true, selfless courage.

We have lost contact, and I wonder whether she has died. I wish I'd told her what she did for me, thanked her for showing me what it means to be truly courageous. But perhaps, if she is in her Heaven, the convicts of Sarah Island are sitting beside her, telling her just that.

—*Maura Bedloe*

Mercy from the Flames

C hristmas morning, I heard technicians dismantling the machines that had kept Sofia, my neighbor in the burn unit for twelve days, alive. I closed my eyes, wishing Sofia well on her journey. I added a prayer for me, to whatever spirits were listening, to heal my own burned face and without the skin grafts a physician had already indicated might be necessary.

Two weeks before Christmas, I'd been at home, preparing an article outline, when my electricity went out during a snowstorm. I lit several candles and sat at my kitchen table, trying to finish the outline.

I woke up in the emergency room of the local hospital.

"You've had a seizure," a doctor told me, "and burned yourself . . . badly."

I was sent that night by ambulance to the nearest

burn unit, in a hospital about fifty miles away. I have epilepsy, and having had epileptic seizures previously, I was no stranger to emergency rooms. But I'd never seriously hurt myself before.

When I have a grand mal seizure, I lose consciousness. My limbs shake, but I'm unable to feel my body's spasms. After I have a seizure, I get an un-me feeling: I don't feel like myself. *What day is it? Where am I? How did I get here?* Then the memories come floating back, like things tossed upon the tide that return to shore with the next wave: *It's Tuesday; there's a storm and the lights go out; I light candles; I'm writing an outline for an article on local farmland protection; I stop for a moment to look at the candlelight flickering on the tablecloth.*

Now, I felt like I was in a bad dream I couldn't wake from. My head and neck were in bandages. A nurse told me I'd suffered second- and third-degree burns on the left side of my head and on my right hand. Nearly two-thirds of the left side of my face and scalp had been burned, from the tip of my nose to my ear. All my hair on that side of my head was burned off. My burned left eyelid was swollen shut. My skin smelled like a rotting hamburger. When I chewed or yawned, my left temple felt like it would come apart.

Why me? I have photosensitive epilepsy, and my eyes are very sensitive to sudden changes in light patterns, like blinking lights. I realized that the flickering of the candles must've triggered the seizure. Still, I asked, *Why me?*

The next day, Michael, my boyfriend, drove nearly sixty miles to the burn unit. I was so glad to see him, yet ashamed.

"I must look horrible," I said.

"I almost lost you," he said, squeezing my hand. "You mean more to me than ever."

I felt very grateful for his words.

"I still don't know how I got here."

Michael sat next to me on the bed. "Your upstairs neighbor, Ray, told me that he smelled hair burning. He said he recognized the smell from his days in the Army. So he ran downstairs, broke through the back door, found you, and called 911."

How kind of him, I thought. We had only a nodding acquaintance. Yet, I was angry, too—at myself.

Regardless, the nurses, the doctors, and Michael told me I was lucky. Lucky that Ray had been home. Lucky that my right thumb had somehow escaped injury and, though my four fingers were bandaged like a snowball, I had enough dexterity to write, brush my teeth, and eat with a fork. Lucky that the vision in both my eyes hadn't been impaired. Lucky to be alive.

"Lucky in my unluckiness," I'd mutter.

It would take a while for me to see it otherwise. One afternoon after Carol, one of my favorite nurses, had given me pain medication, I said, "I can't decide whether my body's reaching the flames during my seizure was just bad luck, or whether my karma, my mind-set, caused it, and this mess is essentially my fault."

Carol was blunt. "If you keep blaming yourself," she insisted, "you'll just waste your life. Instead, why don't you ask yourself, 'What's next?'"

A week after I'd been admitted, I forced myself to look at my bandaged head in the chrome paper towel dispenser next to the bathroom sink. (No mirrors handy there.) My face appeared to be very swollen and very red. My left eyelid looked like a tiny balloon covered with scar tissue. *Why me?*

The only time I was actually in pain was during the showers I took twice daily to prevent infection. An anonymous poet once called pain "the monster with a thousand teeth," and I can't describe any better the stinging, reverberating sensation of stubbly washcloth rubbing against exposed nerve endings. When a nurse scrubbed away the damaged tissue on my eyelid, ear, or forehead, I'd usually jerk my head away like a helpless animal. The Demerol injected into my buttocks before each shower wasn't enough to assuage the pain.

"Try screaming," one of the nurses suggested. "A lot of the men do."

But I couldn't. I strove to absorb the pain, to

move toward, not away from, it. I'd repeat, "It's healing, it's healing," over and over to myself during those showers. I'd imagine I was underwater, watching sea fans gently sway and clownfish glide by.

When Dawn, the youngest nurse in the burn unit, washed me, she'd say, "I'm going to do your ear now," or "I'm at the top of your head." I loved her for telling me this. Somehow, knowing where her hand would land next, I could better brace myself for the pain.

On my way to and from the showers, I'd pass Sofia's room. There were several other patients in the burn unit, but we didn't see much of each other. Sofia was the only one I knew anything about or even saw. She was eighty years old, Carol told me, and had burned herself horribly in her kitchen.

Sofia lay nearly comatose in her bed, mouth open, eyes closed, IV in her arm, tubes in her throat and rectum, a dialysis machine running next to the respirator.

"A few days ago," Carol told me, "Sofia had almost no heartbeat, but the doctors raised it with medication."

Sometimes, I'd stand at Sofia's door, thinking of my mother, who'd been surrounded by the same daunting equipment after a stroke that eventually killed her.

"Sofia," I whispered, "why can't they let you go?"

A few days before Christmas, new skin had

started to replace the scar tissue on my hand; my knuckles now looked only severely sunburned. I eagerly worked with the hospital's occupational therapist, doing exercises—making fists, picking up pennies, using a power grip—to make my hand flexible as new skin grew in.

Yet, not much I did seemed to affect my face's healing. While I was exercising my hand one morning, the occupational therapist told me about the rigors of skin grafting.

"You might be bed-bound for days afterward," she said, "and you might have to undergo more than one skin grafting." To keep the new skin from growing in puffy, she explained, I'd have to wear a pressure garment, a nylon-spandex glove, on my hand and a pressure garment mask, resembling the stockings bank robbers wear, on my face twenty-three hours a day, for at least six months.

I thought about foregoing the skin grafting. After all, it was expensive and I had no health insurance. Maybe the doctor was wrong when he'd warned that the left side of my face would never again look like my right side. Maybe my skin would heal on its own. And even if my face was red, bumpy, and grotesque-looking, perhaps I should accept ugliness as my inevitable fate.

Michael was horrified. "We're not talking about blacktopping the Long Island Expressway," he chided me, "or doing an aluminum siding job. This is your face."

By Christmas Eve, I could scratch the back of my ear. By then, the nurses would let me undo my hand and head bandages by myself; I unwound them slowly, millimeter by millimeter, the anti-bacterial ointment coming off like taffy. During my evening shower on Christmas Eve, I hummed "I'll Be Home for Christmas" as Carol rubbed scar tissue off my forehead. She told me how much I'd improved.

"Honey," she said, "the night you came in here, you looked like a prizefighter."

Later, I saw several doctors gathered around Sofia. "Her blood gas is awful," I heard Carol say, "and her lungs are full of fluid."

I lay down on my bed and turned out the lights. Carols and madrigals from the radio at the nurses' station played softly. The music brought me the soft reminiscences of childhood Christmases: helping my mother bake *chrushik* (Polish pastries), opening our presents on Christmas Eve, going to midnight mass wearing my new red boots. That night as I fell asleep, I longed to feel balanced and held, like a yolk that is simultaneously buoyed and contained within an eggshell.

I awoke hours later. The burn unit was quiet, except for Carol in the next room, talking to Sofia. I strained to hear her words.

"Sofia," Carol said, "you have to make a choice between living and dying. We love you," Carol assured her, "and whatever you choose, everyone will help you."

Then Carol sang to her for several minutes, a gospel tune, in her sweet soprano voice. It was the voice of love, of grace and protection. I'm sure Carol didn't mean for anyone else to hear her, so I felt like an intruder, yet somehow I also felt loved.

Sofia died before dawn. I never saw her body; I just heard people moving equipment and disinfecting the room, readying it for an infant burned in a house fire. Michael arrived at noon, with gifts. We hugged and kissed. I felt very grateful for his kindness, his love. We discussed living together, of perhaps moving to upstate New York or Vermont. Slowly, I could feel myself regaining my equilibrium. Suddenly, my life felt full of possibilities.

But my Christmas wasn't over; there were still more gifts to come. The following morning, the plastic surgeon, a vibrant, sympathetic woman I instantly trusted, examined my face.

"The skin on your face is growing in nice and pink," she said. "It won't need a grafting. Neither will your hand."

Cautiously hopeful, I said, "But the doctor sounded so sure."

"Most doctors are so eager to close things up," she said, "but even though it takes longer, it's always better if the skin grows in itself." She assured me that if she was wrong and I did need grafting, it could always be done later—and I wouldn't have to wear a mask pressure garment on my face.

My unlikely prayer had been answered. Astonished and buoyed by her pronouncement, I telephoned Michael with the good news.

"Didn't I tell you?" he said. "You are lucky!"

Right then, I felt the courage to look at my bare head in the chrome towel dispenser. I actually recognized myself. My left ear looked a little chewed up, and the side of my face was nearly orange and ridged with scar tissue, but new pink skin was peeking through. The hair on my left side had grown to Schnauzer length, and on my unburned side it lay shaggy on my earlobe. Though half of my left eyebrow was burned off, my left eye was now fully open.

As soon as I get out of here, I thought, *I should tattoo the skin where half of my eyebrow is missing: a grapevine, perhaps, or a mermaid. Maybe dye one side of my hair green, the other side purple or magenta. Maybe even get a nose ring.*

"All right," I said aloud. "Maybe I am just a little bit lucky." And though I had no immediate answer, finally I could ask, "What's next?"

—Patricia A. Murphy

The Promise of Indiana

Neither the deep-set brown eyes, the girlish giggle, nor the imperfect but sincere smile suggest that her life has ever been anything less than happy and secure. To hear her tell her story—sitting across from me at an upscale salon in San Marino on a Saturday morning—the events of nearly a quarter century ago seem as far removed from the present as the very jungles of Malaysia in which they transpired.

The other clients—silver-haired and bejeweled women whom I have nicknamed "The Mavens"—pay little attention to our twice-monthly chats. They are there strictly for the upkeep of their fingers and toes, dismissive of the notion that the staff of hard-working, black-haired foreigners in pink smocks would have anything of merit to contribute to a conversation. To these well-heeled patrons, the sound of the Vietnamese language is offensive, a condition that some equate with stupidity or a willful stubbornness against embracing American ways. Only a handful among the stylish clients, most of them younger, look beyond the smock and the job and the shyness to see the courage and determination that brought these women so many miles from the country of their birth.

She was only twelve at the time, living in her native Vietnam with her mother and a younger brother. Her father, exercising his responsibility as the family breadwinner, had taken leave of them six weeks before to join a brother in Indiana who had promised him work as an entry-level machinist at a factory.

Minimum wage. Maximum hope.

"You couldn't all go with him?" I ask, finding it disconcerting that nuclear families couldn't be kept together for what had to be a harrowing journey.

She shakes her head, offering the carefully measured response of one who still finds English a flummoxing way to communicate. "It was not done that way," she explains.

The daunting expense of four people starting a new life all at once was further compounded by her uncle's reluctance to sponsor more than one relative at a time in his newly adopted community. Resentment against Vietnamese immigrants had not abated in the years following American withdrawal from their homeland. Already, she tells me with a blush of self-consciousness, her uncle had moved twice until he'd found a neighborhood that was tolerant of his origins.

"My father would send for us as soon as he could," she says. "Until then, the only thing we could do was wait."

It is one thing to wait to be reunited with a loved one in the same house, which you all once shared as a family. It is quite another to be displaced from your home while the family is still separated by thousands of miles. Her father had not yet been gone three months when financial conditions stemming from her little brother's need for emergency medical treatment forced them to move into another relative's cramped apartment just outside of Saigon.

The second night, she awoke to find a male cousin, seventeen, trying to get in bed with her. The screams that brought her mother running in from where she slept on the kitchen floor elicited only laughter from their host. "She should get used to it," he said, mincing no words that prostitution was her inevitable destiny.

"Get your things," she remembered her mother telling her. "We leave tonight."

Even if she hadn't been too frightened to ask where they were going, she understands in retrospect what her mother would have replied: "I don't know."

In the weeks that followed, they moved from one place to the next. She explains with a pained giggle,

"It was good I did not have too many possessions."
Her remark reminds me of the envy I used to feel in
my twenties for fellow actors who could seemingly
transport all of their worldly possessions in a backpack. Even a backpack, I think, would have seemed
a treasure in itself to this young woman.

Her changing preteen body frightened her, and
her mother was too embarrassed to explain why. She
was not the only one, however, whose changing body
brought feelings of fear and anxiety. Her mother's
waist had begun to thicken, a condition that seemed
curious in light of what little food they ate. One day,
her mother asked her to mind her little brother while
she went to see someone. When she came back, she
was pale and sickly. It would not be until many years
later that she revealed to both of her children that it
would have been a cruelty to bring a third child into
the world when she could hardly provide for the ones
she had.

"What about your father?" I ask. "Was he writing
letters?"

She shakes her head. Not only was English difficult for him but he had to rely on his brother to both
translate what he wanted to say and take the letters
to the post office for him. The friction between them
increased, especially when their mutual employer
deemed her father a more productive worker than
the relative who had sponsored him. Though this

recognition brought with it an increase in pay and responsibility, the first thing he had to do was put it toward a different place to live, one on a bus route, because the jealous uncle also refused to give him a ride to work anymore.

Meanwhile, the homes of relatives with whom his family could stay back in Vietnam diminished. With multiple generations residing beneath one roof, the presence of three more was not welcome. In desperation, her mother sought help from a man who was rumored to have connections to "safe houses" where they could await word from her father in America. For the equivalent of sixty American dollars—"a fortune," she describes it—he would take them to Malaysia, promising the mother a job and both of her children a place in school.

Though he kept his word about getting them into Malaysia, he disappeared shortly thereafter.

"At first my mother thought our savior had come to harm," she says. Her mother soon realized that she and her children were the only ones who had been harmed.

Literally cast adrift in a country that was not only bewildering but hostile, they had no idea how they were to survive, much less how her father would ever find them now that they had left the borders of Vietnam. She remembers her mother waking her up after only a few hours of sleep in an alley. "We will go to the jungle," she said. "We will be safer there."

As someone who has always lived in large cities, I find this decision confusing and say so. "What about wild animals?" I ask. "What about venomous snakes? Weren't you afraid?"

Her dark eyes sparkle as if keeping a secret. "There was more to fear," she says, "if we stayed where we were." In the city they were at risk of exploitation, violence, and disease, and they had heard terrifying rumors of "organ harvesters," which suggested that their value as human beings was regarded as much higher if they were dead.

Her mother, she went on, had been raised in the countryside prior to her marriage at age fourteen. Nature had been her only classroom, teaching her which plants and insects were edible, how to build a makeshift shelter in bad weather, and how to recognize the warning signs of trespass. For however long they might have to keep themselves hidden in the jungles, she would teach these skills to her children.

They were not alone in choosing this route of survival. Others—many from their own country— hid there as well. Nor were all of those in hiding innocent victims; some preyed upon the other refugees, stealing from and even killing them.

"Some left a trail of blood and would leave more if they knew you were alone," she tells me. She and her brother were taught to run fast and to never, ever return to the lean-to if they thought they were being followed by someone who might kill them and take all of their things.

Nearly a year and a half passed. Only when she shared her story with another girl she'd met—a few years older—did a new anxiety set in.

"She laughed at me," she says. "She told me my father probably had a new woman in this place called Indiana and was keeping her belly full of babies he cared about more than me."

Sadly, the convenient lack of a paper trail and the temptation to disavow one's prior life are not uncommon among Third World immigrants. When family members have no way of learning the bread-winner's fate and no means to acquire a sponsor so that they might immigrate themselves, they are consigned to remain in their homelands forever.

"I knew my father would not do that," she declares with a sparkle of pride. "He would keep his promise to us."

"But how?" I ask. Regardless of the man's honorable intentions, how would he know where to locate them?

She stops working on my nails a moment to try to express something with her hands, her slender fingers splayed. "It is a bridge of lace," she explains, "one thread connected to all others and yet its own design."

I find myself wondering if the word she is seeking

is "network," but I'm too enchanted by her mimed description and poetic choice of words to interrupt.

"If one means to hide in the jungles forever," she continues, "they will not be found at any price." Those who do have a need for discovery and let those wishes be known, however, become part of a primitive communications system that predates cell phones, pagers, and e-mail. It is a fragile system of messaging that relies completely on the trust and accuracy of others. In the case of my dark-haired friend at the salon, it is also a system that works.

Nearly two years to the very day that her father left for the United States, word finally came that he had saved enough money to send for them. Six months later—via the Philippines, where the trio underwent quarantine and a requisite orientation to American ways—the family was once more reunited. Indiana—as magical to her young eyes as Oz—was in the middle of its worst winter.

"My mother cursed the snow," she says with a laugh. "She told my father that if we didn't move to California, she would take us back to Vietnam!" Too overjoyed to deny his wife's wish, he set in motion a plan to relocate them to an equally mythical place called Hollywood a few months later.

I compliment her on the courage that kept them going for two years of living in limbo and jeopardy, having no idea what their future might hold. She shakes her head, denying that their bravery was anything special.

"You cannot have courage unless you have faith," she says. "And faith alone—the dream of coming to live in a place called Indiana—is nothing until it is all you have left."

—*Christina Hamlett*

Of Silk and Steel

We sat together in the living room, surrounded by enough snapshots to paper all the walls in the entire house. But all of them mattered, because they were freeze-frame moments of my mom's lifetime.

At eighty-six, my mom was writing her life story and wanted to include pictures. Over the years, the photos had found their way into albums, boxes, bags, and envelopes. Sorting through them was a task of epic proportions.

That led to an epiphany.

I'm forty-something and had assumed I knew pretty much everything there was to know about Mom. I was wrong.

In the early 1950s, Mom lived in a settlement of cabins, lean-tos, and small homes built from scraps salvaged and nailed in place around Anchorage.

Alaska was still an untamed territory. Housing was makeshift, and people were sturdy. Wood had to be chopped, water carried. All the while, the silent snow fell, drifted, deepened.

Mom, or rather, Annie, who was not yet a mom then, was home alone. Her husband, Mark, was at work, flying to God-knows-where as a bush pilot.

Suddenly, screams cut through the quiet and didn't stop. Annie ran out into the snowy yard, and a quick look in each direction settled it: Black smoke billowed from the two-story home a block away. Annie ran toward it. The woman's screams drew more neighbors.

But Annie was intent, searching for two small faces. "Where are the children?" she asked the frantic woman.

"They're in the house, my babies are in the house," the woman shrieked, sobbing and wringing her hands.

There was no time to think about what to do, only time to act. Mom's heart took charge of her feet. One, two—the porch steps were no obstacle to her flying footsteps. Black smoke choked the dark rooms and her own fear of fire felt suffocating, but she had no time to waste—Annie had to find the children.

She couldn't see. She navigated by feel, colliding with walls, tumbling up stairs. A dainty woman, she bruised easily, still she pressed on through the thickening blackness until she found the infant and then the toddler, both too frightened to move. She bundled a baby under each arm and threaded her way back down the darkened staircase, pressing against the inside wall to keep from falling to the floor below. Roiling clouds of murky black smoke belched from the burning furnace, right at the bottom of the stairs. Edging past it with her precious burdens, she finally stumbled out onto the porch, into the stark brightness of a snowscape at midday and the waiting arms of panic-stricken neighbors and a fear-paralyzed mother.

She had never before told this story, not once. I couldn't believe she wouldn't have at least mentioned it. Before then, I had always thought of her as the typical den mother, room mother, seamstress, cook, baker, and general "my Mom will do it" type of superheroine.

To me, she's always been June Cleaver with a bit of an attitude. At that moment, I realized that she hadn't shared with me every detail about every road she has ever traveled. And that somewhere in her drawer of dainty lingerie, she had stashed at least one set of Wonder Woman Underoos.

I pressed her about it: Why hadn't she told me about this before? She smiled and shook her head, just a little, said it was no big deal, that she'd only done what anyone else would've done.

I disagree, and so would any of those who had stood in that snowy front yard all those decades ago. My mom did what no one else, at that place and time, was willing or able to do. On that unsung day in Alaska, two precious lives hung by a single thread. Fortunately, that thread is the sturdy stuff from which my mother's character is knit.

I'd hang my own life on that thread any day of the week.

—*Christy A. Caballero*

You Got Beat by a Girl

At five feet, one inch tall, I am hardly intimidating as an individual, let alone as an ice hockey goalie. My whole body can fit in my equipment bag, with room to spare, and when I carry it, the thirty pounds of goalie armor rattling around inside yanks my confident stride into a crooked-backed waddle. On the ice, crouched and ready to make a save, my head barely clears the cross bar (hockey nets are only four feet high). I look about as threatening as an angry lap dog. But despite being short, what really makes me a spoon among forks is that, 99 times out of 100, I'm the only woman on the ice.

About two weeks into my budding hockey "career," I went to my first pickup (an informal scrimmage where anyone can sign up and play). I needed as much practice as I could get and pickup hockey, I was told, was a good source.

Being the new goalie on the block, I was a bit self-conscious. I embarrass easily, so my greatest challenge was not chickening out. At twenty-four years old, I didn't have the fearlessness of a child, and like all beginners, I was bound to make plenty of mistakes. But you have to start somewhere, and I just tried to not let it bother me too much.

The psychological key in most sports is to feign confidence regardless of how you actually feel—fake it 'til you make it. "Walk in like you own the place," I was once told, so I took a deep breath and strode into the rink like I'd been born right there on the skate rental counter. Unfortunately, my heavy-bag waddle did nothing to toughen up my first impression. It was obvious to anyone paying attention that I was new to the rink, new to the sport, and the only girl in the place.

I headed to the locker rooms and excused my way through burly, hairy, half-dressed male hockey players, until I found a clear area to suit up. The guys didn't look at me, and I didn't look at them. I'd never been in a locker room before, let alone in one with all guys. No matter; I was there to play hockey, not make friends.

After wriggling into my gear, I lumbered my way to the ice and did a couple of laps to warm up my slightly shaky legs. I skated over to one of the two empty nets and got ready to take some warm-up shots. Like ants to a sugar cube, players gravitated toward my end of the rink, thankful to have something to shoot against other than an empty net—although, being that I was so new, an empty net probably would've posed more of a challenge.

Most of the players weren't concerned with my presence, but one idiot, Jake, kept shooting at my head. His first shot nailed me hard in the forehead, but it didn't faze me. Goalies get hit in the head frequently, and we nobly accept that. But after two more very painful shots to my shoulder and collarbone, I knew something was fishy. He was shooting at my head on purpose, and I wasn't having any of that.

Annoyed, I stopped taking his shots, motioning to any other player than him to shoot. He got the picture that my face was no longer his personal clay pigeon and left to go torment the goalie at the other net. As he skated away, he narrowed his eyes and smirked, thinking he'd succeeded in intimidating me. He hadn't. I stopped taking his shots not because I was scared of Jake or of head injuries, but because any self-respecting goalie would've done the same thing. The nature of our position entails enough abuse; we don't need to tolerate additional pounding from some clod just trying to get our goat. In an actual game, I'll do anything humanly possible to stop a puck, gladly blocking it with my noodle if that's what it takes. But this wasn't an actual game;

it was a pickup, which is supposed to be just for fun.

My composure hid my irritation. I let it go and continued the rest of the pickup without incident. However, next time I saw him, I would be prepared.

At the same Vallco pickup a year later, who should walk onto the ice but Jake. Behind my goalie mask hid a small, devilish grin. I'd been waiting for the day I could teach Jake not to underestimate women—especially this one. With hundreds of hours of training now under my belt, I was a lot better than the first day he'd played against me. It was time to kick his cocky butt.

Recognizing his favorite target—me—he confidently snorted and skated to the bench. He must've been thinking he was going to clobber me, that he'd teach me a lesson for coming back. Maybe he'd shoot for my neck this time and collapse my trachea. Maybe I'd impale him with my stick and impair his ability to have children. Anything could happen. We took our places, opponents for the second time.

My training paid off. I was as fast as, if not faster than, Jake. Several excellent scoring attempts were thwarted by several magnificent saves—all by a small girl who'd been playing only a year against a burly guy who'd been playing far longer. He didn't score once. He did, however, manage to blast me square in the collarbone again, reminding me of the excruciating pain he'd inflicted a year prior. The important thing is, the puck didn't go in.

As he skated to the bench at the end of the scrimmage, Jake glared at me over his shoulder, clearly defeated, then shook his head and called me something unpleasant under his breath. I beamed with vengeful pride, feeling like I'd just crushed an enemy soldier. Then, as if being shown up by a yearling wasn't humbling enough, a friend of mine salted the wound by belting out the universal guy phrase of shame: "You got beat by a girl!"

A week later, at a San Jose Sharks game, I was on my way to the concessions during intermission. Halfway there, I spotted Jake. I'd never seen him in street clothes; he was actually kind of cute. I tried to slip past him unnoticed, wanting to forget that my nemesis and I were again sharing airspace. Just when I thought I'd managed to go undetected, I heard a friendly, "Hey, Danielle!" His cordial acknowledgment caught me way off guard. I was slightly shocked and definitely suspicious, but played it cool and returned an unassuming, "Hey, Jake." I kept on walking, not sure whether he wanted me to stop and converse, and too distrustful to wait and find out. I'd gauge his sincerity on the ice.

Sure enough, at pickup he was still nice to me. The rivalry was over. We had our first pleasant conversation and have been friends ever since.

Recently I asked him about the original head-hunting incident. I was curious whether he had intentionally shot at my head because I was a girl or whether he was a universal creep.

He laughed. "Yeah, it was because you're a girl," he said.

So I asked him why he'd been such a jerk.

"I just wanted to see if I could scare you off." He went on to say that he didn't think I could cut it. "But you didn't back down, and you're a great goalie, so I gave up."

I playfully punched him in the arm, hard, a belated payback.

Most men have no qualms about women in hockey, and then there are guys like Jake. Jake was the first, but not the last, guy who's gone out of his way to rattle me, and each time I meet up with one, I do the same thing. I hit them where it really hurts—on the scoreboard. To some men, being out-played by a woman is more painful than anything I could do to them physically. It's the same every time. They see me, they underestimate me, I stone them, they respect me. I take the lumps because I love hockey, and if it helps prevent the next female hockey player who comes along from having to get belted in the face to be accepted, it only makes my bruises all the more worth it.

—Danielle deLeon

All Creatures Great and Small

My daughter, Jill, paused halfway down our front steps. She turned and said, "Mom, will you sing to me? Will you hold me and sing like you used to when I was a little girl?"

Her husband and two little stepdaughters stopped on the sidewalk and looked back.

I always sang to my kids when they were young. Jill and her older brother shared a bedroom, and I knelt between them, holding one's hand and stroking the blond head of the other. And I sang. I crooned through "Dona, Dona" and "Kumbaya." I swayed in rhythm to "Swing Low, Sweet Chariot." I never missed a verse of "Hush Little Baby." I made up songs, too, a habit that drove my husband crazy. On nights I was out, the kids begged, "Sing 'The Horse Broke the Fence,' Daddy," or "No, we want 'The Big Wheel' song." And they didn't mean "Proud Mary," which he might have managed, although he really couldn't carry a tune even when he knew the words.

The kids and I always finished with "All Things Bright and Beautiful," and I watched their active bodies quiet and their eyes grow dreamy as they imagined the purple-headed mountains and the ripe fruit in the garden of the old hymn. By the time I warbled my way through the refrain for the last time, one of them had usually twitched and fallen asleep.

As Jill grew from child to adult, it became apparent that she had inherited her father's trouble carrying a melody. She cuddles with her girls every night and reads to them, but she just can't sing to them.

I baby-sat for our granddaughters not long ago. After I tucked them into our king-size bed, I sang "Dona, Dona," "Kumbaya," and all the others. Hannah, the six-year-old, lay still as a stone, gazing at the ceiling. Four-year-old Brianna came forward on hands and knees, staring into my eyes from so close that her features blurred. In the dim light drifting through the open door, I saw her lips half open, glistening. Trancelike, she held perfectly still, listening as if she wanted to inhale the songs directly from my mouth.

It was a few days later that Jill asked me to sing to her. She said, "The girls talked about your singing, Mom, and it brought back all the memories. I remember my cool pillow and your hand on my hair. I remember my nightgown with the sunbonnet dolls on it and the pink ice cream cone quilt you made. And the fish mobile and my toy puppy with the music box. Sometimes I woke up when you kissed me one last time."

That's when she turned and asked, "Mom, will you sing to me again?"

Her husband stood beneath the street lamp with a child balanced on each hip. Her father and brothers stood behind me, illuminated by the porch light.

She's very tall, this girl of mine. Standing on the step below me, she still had to stoop to put her head against my chest. I wrapped my fingers in her long hair, and she wound her arms around my waist.

"What shall I sing, Jill?" I asked.

"You know, Mom," she said, looking up and smiling.

"'All Things Bright and Beautiful'?"

"Of course." She snuggled closer. "All the verses."

I kissed the top of her head and began to sing.

> *All things bright and beautiful,*
> *All creatures great and small . . .**

I swallowed a lump in my throat and stroked her back as I continued through the verses. Off-key, she joined in.

Jill began to cry, and so did I, but the words still flowed as my mind traveled back over the years. I remembered her birth, how ecstatic I'd been to have a daughter, what an easy child she was, her habit of rescuing small animals, championing the underdog, and befriending the outcast. I remembered how she loved to please others—and still does.

This girl of mine who married young and took on the daunting task of raising another woman's children is no longer under my wing. She's a young woman now, and I can no longer tuck the ice cream cone quilt around her shoulders each night. I cannot protect her from pain, from hurt, from mature responsibilities. I can't make growing up any easier for her.

Jill's tears soaked through my T-shirt and mine dropped to her bowed head. She clung tightly, and then looked up into my face.

"The purple headed mountains. Don't forget the purple headed mountains," she whispered, staring at me through the dim light just as Brianna had a few nights earlier, drinking in the words, the memories, and the song. Drinking in my love.

> *The purple headed mountains,*
> *The river running by . . .**

My voice cracked, and I could sing no more. We stood locked together on the stairs.

I know the enormity of the task she's taken on is sometimes almost more than she can handle. I know how hard she's working to create a home of the house she now lives in. Cradling her in maternal love, allowing her to remember falling asleep to a mother's singing—it was the best I could offer her that night.

Jill squeezed me tightly and then turned toward her husband and stepdaughters. Her dad hugged me as I watched her settle the girls into the backseat of their car. Then I heard the hymn again. I strained my ears, listening. Jill was humming the refrain. As they pulled away from the curb, Brianna's thin, childish voice burbled from the open car window:

> *All things wise and wonderful,*
> *The Lord God made them all.**

—Peggy Vincent

*"All Things Bright and Beautiful," Cecil F. Alexander, *Hymns for Children*, 1848.

Reinventing Myself

At age twenty-two, I was Shakespeare's Juliet and married my Romeo. This action caused my usually loving parents to take down my picture and to pack away every gift I had ever given them. My sensitive new husband, the person who had been my best friend for the previous four years, was Catholic. My immediate family and very large extended family were conservative, evangelical Christians, and they were certain I had made a terrible mistake.

Although I missed my family and could never quite shake the ache of hurting my parents, I threw myself into my new life. I loved being a wife, and soon parenting became my joy. We had three children in a row, each born three years apart—Jeff, Joan, and Jim—and several years later added our fourth and only adopted child, Jill, a tiny four-year-old girl who had been badly abused. The five of us worked together to create a safe world for Jill. It was only coincidence that our fourth child also had a J name, but the children saw it as proof that they were meant to be a team.

Weekdays during the school year, I took the children swimming when they returned home from school and I from my teaching job. When they were little I tossed them into the water and taught them to bob down and "look for fishes." When they were older we raced each other in the pool, and when they started to outpace me, they did back flips at the end of the pool while I swam my laps.

Weekends in the winter the six of us skied. My husband, Mike, and the children performed daredevil tricks, while I skied steadily and burst with pride at their feats. As a family we volunteered at the soup kitchen, worked with refugees, and filled in the front row in church. We were one of the good families. Teacher conferences always went well, we had many friends, and my parents admitted to my friends that they were proud of me.

But secretly, behind closed doors, something was happening in my family that I didn't understand. My husband had evolved into someone I no longer recognized. One moment he would be moody and impossible to please. The next, the phone would ring and Mike would sound happy and normal as he talked to the person on the other end. More and more he blamed the children and me for his unhappiness. But no matter what we did or didn't do, nothing kept him happy for long. Yet, in public, Mike would tell the children and me that he loved us deeply and that we were the most important thing in his life.

Unable to admit that we weren't the perfect family we appeared to be, I slid into a silent depression, which I tried to hide, and I worried about my children. When I did try to talk to one of my close friends, she thought I was being unfairly hard on my husband. Years of depression finally led me to see a counselor. After a few sessions alone with her, she told me to come in with Mike. I brought him to the next session, and he turned on the charm. The counselor said she couldn't see any real problems in my life. She offered me drugs to control what she saw as *my* problem. I turned down the offer and continued to struggle on my own.

Mike had always been a risk taker, but in recent years it had escalated. His wild driving caused two serious accidents. Both times his cars were the only ones involved, and though they were demolished, he miraculously escaped serious injury. His business decisions became irrational. In addition to his erratic behavior, it became impossible to reason with him and to discuss our growing problems. Soon after our oldest son left for the Navy, we lost our home. The five of us remaining in the home ended up in an ugly two-bedroom apartment in a building that Mike had purchased to remodel. As always, Mike put up a good face for the rest of the world. No one seemed to suspect that we were in turmoil.

Late one night after one more fight about nothing, I begged Mike to tell me what was really wrong. I pleaded with him. I said I was going crazy. He nodded in agreement. Then he sat quietly, and for more than an hour he opened up and told the truth.

As he talked, the world as I knew it disintegrated, never to return. The craziness had an explanation, but it was one I never could have expected and didn't want to hear.

My Romeo had never loved me. He was a gay man who desperately wanted to be straight. He said all the right words—complimenting me on my appearance, professing his attraction to me, sharing "girlie" jokes with other guys—but his secret was causing him to lose his mind. He also had become addicted to gambling. Our money was gone, and we were deeply in debt.

For one long year, as we visited counselor after counselor, I kept his secret. Though neither of us believed in divorce, we eventually saw that we had no choice. We told the children the truth, and ended our marriage. We had been married for twenty-four years. The year that followed was a nightmare.

The children had requested that we keep silent abut the reason for the end of our marriage until they'd had time to adjust and heal. I found that when I did confide in someone, that person frequently became uncomfortable and the friendship disappeared.

I saw an ad in the paper for a support group for the former spouses of "outed" gays and lesbians. I attended the group, which was led by a woman who had been divorced for fourteen years and was still deeply grieving. In fact, all of the members were having difficulty going on with their lives. Their sense of self had been destroyed. I did not go back to the group.

Jeff, my oldest, found supportive, open friends in the Navy. Joan, far from home and a sophomore in college, discovered that a close friend was dealing with the same problem; with her friend's support, Joan, too, healed. But my two youngest were not doing as well.

Jim, who had been Mr. Popular at his large high school, dropped out of school activities and became totally absorbed in his job as a radio disc jockey. His best friend had let his tongue slip and jokingly revealed to their friends that Jim's father was gay. Jim couldn't deal with the teasing that resulted. The radio station was a business. They happily let this talented high school student work forty or fifty hours a week, completely unaware that he was drowning in pain and almost destroying his educational future.

When I went to fall conferences, Jill's teacher indignantly informed me that Jill had told a little boy in her class that her daddy didn't live with her anymore because he is gay. Incensed, the teacher told me how upset the boy's parents were and that I would have to "do something with Jill." "After all," the teacher continued, her voice haughty and hard, "everyone knows that gay people don't have children. What could possibly cause Jill to fabricate such a story? She is upsetting a 'normal' child. Her outlandish stories cannot be tolerated."

I did not defend my child. That truth haunts me to this day. My own agony was so deep I could not stand up to the teacher. My daughter deserved a mother with energy, one who could muster righteous indignation. Maybe she should have been moved to another class. Above all, Jill had deserved to be defended and I could not do it. I did go home and hug her, but that hug was all I had to offer.

The next week I became ill, so ill I could not even crawl from my bed. I called a friend to help in small ways with Jill, but other than that, my two youngest were on their own. In the evenings, when I was alone with them, they stayed in front of the television and would not come to me. I would plead for one of them to bring me a cup of tea, but they were deaf to me. Their mother was weak, and they were breaking inside. They did not need a weak mother, they needed a rock.

I got on the phone and pleaded until I found a counselor my insurance would cover who would see us, not in two months, not in one month, but *now*.

I prayed for courage. I needed courage to reinvent myself, one day at a time. I needed to be strong. I needed to discover my inner passions and to know who I am. I had spent so many years taking care of Mike, I no longer knew what my own interests were. Little by little, that courage came. Moment by moment, I grew stronger. I revived my long-ago dream of being a writer, and as I wrote, I began to heal.

Several years later, all four of my children had T-shirts printed that said, "We Love Our Gay Dad," and they flew to Washington, D.C., to march with him in the Gay Pride parade. The following month they joined me at one of my many public readings, where I was receiving an award for my writing. The event was attended by my parents, children, students, colleagues, and my darling new husband. We have now been married six years.

Today, my son Jeff has a wonderful job, and he and his wife are awaiting the arrival of their first child. My daughter Joan and her husband are overseas on a Peace Corps mission, and my son Jim is an outstanding college student. Mike is doing well.

Best of all, last week I watched my youngest, Jill, graduate from high school with her head held high. This morning I cried as she boarded an airplane to begin basic training with the Air Force.

After wiping away my tears, I opened this morning's paper. A woman wrote to "Dear Abby" about her grief in discovering that her husband of thirty years is gay. The woman feels that her life is over.

I sat down and wrote the woman a letter. It says, in part, "Have the courage to reinvent yourself. You can do it. Life will be better than you can possibly imagine."

—*Janet Lindstrom (a pseudonym)*

Moving Grandma West

Seen from the air, Aberdeen, South Dakota, is flat in all directions. In February the land is white-gray, like the inside of an old freezer. Train tracks crisscross the city. Small wood frame and brick houses line the streets. Dark tree branches claw the sky. As we make our final descent, I look to my step-mother, Carla, and make a series of silent prayers: *Let our tiny plane set down safely. Let this trip go easily. Let my father be okay. Let me not cry too much.*

We have come to Aberdeen to move my grand-mother to New Mexico. She is my father's mother, and unlike my dad, she has never left the place of her birth. We thought she never would. After the death of my grandfather, we invited her several times to move to Albuquerque; the answer was always no. This stubbornness is not born from a lack of love. It's just that, in her world, there is no room for change.

My grandmother does not dance. She does not dance because she never has. That is the way it is.

The thing that got Grandma Rose to change her mind is that my father, at the age of fifty-eight, has been diagnosed with Alzheimer's disease. She is moving to New Mexico to look after her only child.

When we enter Grandma's apartment, she hugs me quickly.

"Are you hungry?" she asks. "Are you warm enough?"

A man in a baseball cap and denim jacket pushes himself out of a rocker and stretches out a hand. He is my dad's cousin, Bill.

"So, you're the daughter," he says.

"Uh, yeah."

"You gonna put yer dad in a home?" His eyes grow beady. "You know, I got the same thing. I just ain't been diagnosed yet. 'Course, your dad's always been crazy up here." He taps his head with a thick finger. "So, you gonna put him in a home?"

I want to have a strong, adult answer. I want to ask about his feelings of inadequacy. I want to bring up the frustration of being trapped in a small town, of watching his cousin live a life of creativity and adventure. I want to be smart and insightful, but, instead, I spew, "What kind of sicko question is that?"

I whirl into the kitchen, lean over the sink, and run water over my trembling hands.

From the living room, I hear Bill laugh, say he should be going. I stay in the kitchen until I hear the front door close. Carla comes to my side.

"I guess I wasn't really ready for that question," I admit.

Carla squeezes my shoulder. "Your dad says he was always a jackass."

We go to dinner at a place called The Flame, which has been around since my dad was a rebellious teen. Grandma orders a chicken sandwich; Carla and I order steaks, baked potatoes, and red wine.

"You know," Carla says, "I never eat red meat, but it seems sort of . . . appropriate."

"Yep," I agree, raising my glass. "To meat."

"I never had but one boyfriend," Grandma says.

Carla and I look at each other in surprise. We are not used to Grandma's sudden and random bursts of information.

"That was Grandpa, right?" I ask.

"I made him wait four years before we married."

"Why?" Carla and I say together.

"He wanted to save some money, to get us a place and some furniture."

When I was ten, I spent my birthday money from Grandma on a book of poetry by Shel Silverstein. I included some carefully copied poems in my thank-you note. She wrote back that she didn't read much poetry but Grandpa had written some poems for her when they were courting. I wonder how many poems he wrote, what they were about, and where they are now. Are they packed for the trip to Albuquerque, or have they been lost in all the years in between?

Back outside, Grandma refuses to let me take her arm, though the sidewalk has grown icier.

"I am not feeble," she says. "I am independent. Don't you two forget that."

Grandma has decided that Carla and I will take her bed. When we protest, she explains that the sofa folds out. I do not know if she sleeps. I do know she doesn't change out of the sweatshirt emblazoned with an appliquéd heart and plastic letters that read, "I love you, Auntie Rose."

Carla and I climb into Grandma's bed, both of us trying to leave the other as much space as possible. I have been dreading this moment a little.

"How's Dad?" I ask.

Carla can't even get through a sentence before I start to cry. She cries, too. We talk of money and of care, and I realize that the enormous love I have for my father is more than evenly matched by Carla's love for her husband.

Dishwater pale, the morning comes not a minute too soon. We start with a diner breakfast of doughy muffins, lots of coffee, and a visit with Ruth, Grandma's sister-in-law. Ruth's husband was killed in a car wreck when he was thirty-three. She did not remarry, and simply worked and saved, raising the children with the help of the family.

A widow herself for almost twenty years, Grandma pats Ruth's arm and says, "We're the type of girls who don't marry twice. We'd take the old ones back, but we don't go find more."

After breakfast, the bank is our first stop. Grandma carries all her important papers in a yellow canvas bag bearing a picture of a smiling frog. She remarks a number of times during the day, "It's my money. You don't get none of it. You got your own." We nod, smile, and say, "Yes. Yes."

Next, we head to the mortuary to wrap up the details of Grandma's final resting place. The plot has been paid off for years, death being, to my grandparents, the only real reason to splurge. Once the paperwork is in order, we drive to the cemetery and soon realize that flat brass grave markers are no help when covered by six inches of snow. Where is Grandpa? We scrape off the snow with our feet and find Brown, Drake, and Peterson, but no Ward.

"Are you sure?" we ask.

"I should know where my own husband is," Gram says.

And so we continue until, eventually, all the snow in the area is turned over and Grandpa is still lost. Carla and I seek help in the small, brick cemetery office, where on a wall covered with sheets of graph paper, penciled names in a smudged hand make up a map. We peer at the map and see that, there, across from where we've been looking, is "Ward, Everett."

We head back out to Gram and within a matter of moments we have found Grandpa. We pose for a photo next to the brass plaque. As soon as the shutter snaps, Grandma moves toward the car without a backward glance. I wonder if she is thinking of those four years before they married. Of the poems he wrote her. Of the furniture they moved into their first apartment. Or is she thinking she'd like a sandwich and a cup of milk? That it's colder this winter than the last? I don't know, and I realize I will never know. I come from a closemouthed clan. For not the first time, I wonder at my need to tell stories.

Dad's diagnosis came three weeks ago. Although it does not yet seem real, we are so much more aware that he is at home alone. On the phone that night, Dad tells me he is reading a book about the brain. He tells me to watch out for his cousin Bill.

"I love you," I say.

"I'm mighty fond of you, too," he says, chuckling.

The exchange is one we've shared thousands of times, but now it takes on new weight. How long will he continue to remember this joke? What will I say when he forgets?

My father is fifty-eight years old. Who will walk

me down the aisle, and who will be a grandfather to my children? Dad's illness, like any catastrophe, is something we never expected. I look across the room at my stepmother and my grandmother. The troops are gathering. In Aberdeen, South Dakota, three generations of women are taking their first steps toward acceptance.

"What'll you charge me to wash my hair?" Grandma says.

"It's on the house," I reply.

She disappears into the kitchen. She reappears in a white brassiere and hands me a towel and a bottle of shampoo. Grandma leans over the sink, and I let the tap water flatten the wiry result of a permanent wave she gets every six months from "a girl across town." This is the first time I have seen the skin of her back, the soft dimples in her shoulders, the downy hollow at the base of her neck. This is a place I like to be kissed. Were my grandfather's lips ever pressed to this spot? Did his arms slide around her waist to pull her against him? Because my father exists I know this must have happened once. I want to think that it happened more than once. I want to think that there is something wild and restless in my grandmother. I want, most of all, to see some trace of my passionate father in this still and silent woman.

On our last day in Aberdeen the movers arrive. After only a few trips, the apartment is empty.

Looking dazed, Grandma lowers herself onto the floor and hands me a chocolate bar.

"You know, your Dad's real sick."

I feel attacked by even the slightest reference to my dad's illness. I lean back, trying to contain myself. Grandma pats my hand.

"Eat," she says.

That night is spent with my father's cousin Dick and his wife, Ann. Dick is a cheerful man with graying hair and buckteeth. His limp is the result of the car accident that killed his father.

"Hey," Dick says, "You want to see me make fire from flint and steel?"

In the living room, we watch as Dick places straw and a piece of carbon cloth in the fireplace. He takes a bit of flint from a leather pouch and strikes it against a piece of steel. Sparks fly, Dick blows, his cheeks puffing with effort. The straw catches, then peters out. Dick blows harder, scattering ashes over the carpet.

Ann says, "The minute I get this room clean, Dick's back in here with the flint and steel."

"Here we go," Dick shouts. And there, on the edge of the fireplace, a tiny flame licks at the straw and begins to brighten.

The next morning, Dick and Ann accompany us to the airport. Grandma's lip begins to quiver. She hugs Dick and Ann so tightly that I know she has realized she will never see them again. She hugs them so tightly that for the umpteenth time I wonder if this is right. As we board the plane, Grandma reaches for our hands like a child.

Aberdeen grows small below. Grandma sits with her face pressed to the window and her hand clasped tightly in Carla's. She is crying soundlessly, the tears catching in her glasses and making dark spots on her turquoise coat. Carla tucks a tissue into Grandma's hand and rubs her shaking shoulders.

I realize that we will not return to Aberdeen until we lay Grandma to rest and find her name, written in fresh pencil, on the graph paper map at the cemetery. Grandma does not dance because she never has. She has never traveled; she does not know how to drive. Yet here she is, pulling up stakes so late in the game. Change has brought change. Right now, we can only guess at the transformation my father will undergo. So we must cling to what we know. We know we love him, that love will somehow lead us through one day and then the next. Dad's illness will bring us all to new territory.

Grandma may never learn to dance, but she has the capacity to change. If she can do it, we can, too. We gain altitude, and I send up a little bubble of hope and imagine it catching the sun over the flat, icy land below.

—Tanya Ward Goodman

Where Doves Dare to Fly

It was a bitterly cold January night. Beth glanced at her watch: 4:00 A.M. Three more hours and she could relax. Earlier that evening, a four-year-old and a six-year-old, left alone in their home, had started a fire that had driven Beth, along with police and fire crew, out into the frigid night air. It had taken Beth a while to calm the frightened, though thankfully not seriously harmed, children and then to oversee their hospital checkup and placement in a temporary shelter. The agency's day staff would follow up from there.

Sipping a cup of hot tea in the quiet of her kitchen, Beth tried to calm her jangled nerves. She didn't want to disturb John and her two-year-old daughter, Suzie, who were fast asleep in their bedrooms. For Beth, attempting to sleep was useless. Even if no other child-in-peril calls came in that night, her mind would not let her rest.

Why was she doing this—rescuing other people's abused, neglected, and abandoned children in the middle of the night? True, it was what she had trained for. She wanted to do something useful with her life. She'd chosen night shift because it was important for her to be home with Suzie during the daytime while John was at work, and John could attend to Suzie if she awoke during the night. But the worst always seemed to happen in the darkness, and she wondered whether she'd made the right choice.

The beeper startled her, and her heart began to race, as it always did now. Like Pavlov's dogs, she had become conditioned to respond instantly to the impending drama and risks that each call signaled.

When, as a young idealistic woman from a "nice" middle-class background, she decided to become a social worker, she had no idea of the potential dangers she would face in her work. Soon enough, she heard about the experiences of other child protective services workers whose teeth had been punched out or whose lives had been threatened by the knife-wielding or gun-toting relatives of the endangered children. This was not the image of social work held by most of the people Beth knew. Her friends and family outside the field saw social workers as a bunch of do-gooders who brought baskets of goodies and welcome advice to people who were eternally grateful.

After a short time on the job, Beth's youthful

idealism was tempered with harsh realism. She learned firsthand about the mental and emotional toughness needed to deal with extremely difficult, sometimes heartbreaking, often volatile situations. Rather than being met with open arms and gratitude, she was more frequently met with resentment and hostility. The fear of a situation escalating into violence terrified her. Upon returning from lunch one day, she saw a female worker lying at the bottom of the cement steps of her office building, unable to move. Enraged by the social worker's attempts to keep his four-year-old son in child protective care, the father had pushed the woman down the stairs. An ambulance took her away. Beth never did find out what happened to her.

Colleagues had warned her about what might happen when parents or relatives of abandoned children showed up while social workers were in the process of removing the children from the home. More often than not, the family members were drunk, strung out on drugs, or mentally unstable— powder kegs waiting to blow—and taking their kids into protective custody was often the spark that lit the fuse. Although Beth had never had such an experience, her heart pounded with fearful anticipation of such an altercation whenever her beeper sounded.

"If you anticipate danger, call the police to accompany you," her supervisors told her.

That may sound reasonable and reassuring, but she knew there was no way to accurately predict when a situation might become dangerous. That is particularly true in an emergency situation, when you are unlikely to have had any prior knowledge of or experience dealing with the parties involved.

Beth responded to the number left on her beeper.

"A baby has been left alone at the Winchester Hotel," a woman's raspy voice said. "You'll find her on top of a washing machine near the front lobby." *Click.* The phone line went dead.

The Winchester was in the seediest part of town. Should she call the police? Instinct, or perhaps intuition, propelled her fingers to the phone. For the second time that night, Beth set out alone in the darkness to remove a child from harm's way.

The hotel was a dilapidated old building in a run-down area of the city. During the summer, many homeless and derelicts could be found wandering around and sleeping in doorways and alleys. But this was winter, in Canada, and no one could survive long in the arctic air. Except for a large-framed man walking unsteadily down the street, the slum was deserted. Even in the distance, Beth could see icicles clinging around the man's hairy beard and clouds of his breath hanging in midair. She shivered, despite having the car heater at full blast, and pulled her parka tighter around her.

Time seemed to crawl as she watched nervously for the police to arrive. She knew the likelihood of an angry relative appearing increased with each passing second. In their absence, she could be in and out in a matter of minutes. She couldn't wait any longer and stepped out into the icy air. Although it was the middle of the night, several pairs of eyes turned toward her as she entered the shabby, dimly lit lobby.

"Over there," said a scruffy-looking woman with a raspy voice, pointing to a whimpering bundle that lay like discarded laundry on top of an old washer.

An image of Suzie, safe and warm in her crib, flashed through Beth's mind. She walked over to the child and picked her up. As she turned to leave, a huge hulk of a man, icicles clinging to his unkempt beard, filled the entrance doorway. He lurched forward, and the nauseating stench of alcohol flooded the room. Paralyzed with fear, Beth watched as he staggered menacingly toward her, eyes blazing with fury. His hand reached into his pocket, and a flash of reflected light revealed the blade of a knife. She heard a voice behind her refer to him as "the uncle."

"You ain't takin' no kid outta here!" he shouted, along with a litany of obscenities aimed at Beth. "I'll kill you first!"

The infant began to wail, and Beth crept backward, trembling so much she could hardly hold on to the baby. Beth's mind raced as her eyes searched for a way out. Several onlookers stood passively watching as if the terrifying scene playing out before them was a movie designed for their entertainment.

Two blue uniforms appeared in the doorway. They moved quickly to subdue the man. She almost sank to her knees with relief but managed to keep herself together long enough to express her gratitude and to carry out the rest of her duties, taking the child for the hospital exam and then to the shelter.

When Beth rose late the next day after a restless sleep, her first thoughts were on the baby she had placed. *Who was she? Where were her parents? What would happen to her?* She dressed quickly and drove to the shelter. Baby Kimberly, cradled in the arms of a home care worker, looked up at Beth with big, brown smiling eyes. The woman patiently coaxed a bottle of milk into her mouth while Kimberly playfully shook a toy piggy rattle, squealing gleefully with every *oink-oink* sound it emitted. Again, Beth thought of her own little Suzie and struggled with feelings of compassion mixed with indignation. *How could Kimberly's parents abandon her like a load of dirty laundry? Isn't a safe and nurturing home every child's birthright?* Fate might be indifferent, but Beth could not be. Suddenly, she knew why she had chosen to do this work—and she knew she had made the right choice.

—*Libby Simon*

You've Got to Be Kidding

Those Jewish fellows talked him into it, those men of the world with whom he met every Saturday morning at Gus's steam baths in the basement of the old Royal Alexandra Hotel. Dad was thrilled to be included with Blackie and the others for their Saturday morning routine of melting in rooms of cleansing steam and exhibiting their masculinity in old-world fashion. Gus's invigorating rubdowns were culminated with a short nap before generous platters of corned beef on rye bread sandwiches were delivered along with chopped liver pate, kosher dills, and marinated herrings from a neighborhood delicatessen.

Conversations boasted of business coups, solid stock market bets, wholesale purchases, and complaints of unintentional golf slices. They compared their Florida vacation spots and convinced Dad that

Miami was the place for him, a place where he could escape the Winnipeg winter, soak in the sunshine, and press his feet into the warm, wet sand on the Southern U.S. coast of the Atlantic.

Dad saved his money as best a pensioned spendthrift was able, and one day he surprised Mom with the news that he'd made arrangements for them to leave for Miami the first Sunday in February.

She said, "You've got to be kidding."

But, of course, he wasn't.

My husband and I were expected to visit Mom and Dad on their month-long holiday, just as my brother and his pal had done. And so, we did.

The flight was horrible. On the second leg of our journey, we had to turn back to the Montreal airport and then had to prepare for landing by sitting bent over with our heads between our legs. Occasionally, we would dare to peek through the little oval windows at the brigade of yellow fire trucks below, fully knowing they were gathered there for our benefit. Our descent was devoid of conversation, the silence marked only by the rumble of the engines, the odd baby crying, squeaks from the overhead baggage compartments, and the mutterings of prayer, until the great collective exhale upon landing. Everyone cheered with relief at alighting unscathed.

I was not so cheerful, knowing that my husband and I had to take off again, bound for Miami. But not

until we'd polished off more than a couple of complimentary cocktails and waited out a snowstorm that
moved in to smother the Dorval airport, significantly
delaying all flights. Thinking the storm would be
short-lived, the crew requested we stay on the plane
while mechanics made the necessary repairs to one
of the 747's engines. Flight attendants plied us with
more liquor and then lunch and then supper and
then a multitude of snacks consisting of fancy sandwiches, salted peanuts, and little rolls of LifeSavers.
They opened up the aircraft doors to the blisteringly
cold winds in an effort to refresh the deteriorating
atmosphere within the plane, but that served only to
freeze the unfortunate souls who happened to be sitting near the exits.

Eventually, the doors were closed and the big
silver capsule rolled out onto a long, freshly cleared
runway, as my knuckles took on a deathly white color.

Meanwhile, my parents awaited our arrival. Dad,
of course, took it all in stride. "No news is good
news," he told Mom, as she, after five hours, was
reduced to mumbling threats to airline agents
pleading ignorance over the phone.

Seven hours late, in the sultry dark, our bus
pulled in front of the modest Ocean Gate Motel, a
little clutch of units then situated on South Beach.
Dad's sun-scorched face immediately popped up
from behind a lounge chair beside the brilliantly lit

turquoise pool. He had been chain-smoking and bending the ear of a leathery-skinned, shriveled old man who seemed to be sound asleep. Dad led us with pride to the beachfront unit that he and Mom had called home for the previous two weeks.

But when my parents had arrived, it didn't look like home to Mom. Though the rooms came with maid service, the initial impression of the place did not pass Mom's inspection. She immediately instructed Dad to set the air-conditioner and then sent him in search of her favorite cleaning supplies, including a big jug of chlorine bleach. Meanwhile, she used one of the large bottles of isopropyl alcohol that she'd brought in her carry-on case for disinfecting such things as toilet seats, telephone receivers, door handles, and refrigerator interiors. Before Dad returned, she had unpacked the suitcases, made the bed, plugged in the refrigerator, and was watching her afternoon soap operas.

At 3:00 A.M., they'd awakened to night sweats, convincing Mom they had contracted a dreadful tropical disease . . . until she realized Dad had set the heating/cooling unit in the living room to heat rather than to air-conditioning.

Dad spent that first week riding buses, at times venturing into seedy neighborhoods, talking to anyone willing to listen, and stopping to savor such things as tacos, chili, and fat spicy hotdogs from street carts, open-air cafés, and delis. Mom sewed his name and Florida address into his clothing so that they would know where to send his body should he eat something particularly nasty.

Meals they shared together consisted of sensible food at their oceanfront abode or at Denny's restaurant, where the blue-haired waitresses had clean fingernails and remembered your name after the first visit. They brought bowls of delicious little dill pickles to each table, and every meal came with sweaty glasses of cold, tree-fresh orange juice that tasted as sweet as Kool-Aid.

Though Dad was a proud old Manitoba prairie dog, he definitely had salt water running through his veins. He spent many hours walking the beach, deeply inhaling the sea air, and winking back at the sparkles that danced on the water and reflected from his hazel eyes.

One gusty morning after our arrival, I found my Dad standing uncharacteristically still on the shore, his Hawaiian shirt tucked into the belt set high on his aging torso, his pant legs rolled to the knee exposing one normal leg and one thin and bony. The paralysis suffered from his 1943 war wound had noticeably taken its toll through the years, at times making walking more difficult, withering his leg and bending the fingers of his left hand to a permanent claw. Some days, the metal plate in his head bore down on him with debilitating headaches, but not on that day. That day, he played like a child as he gathered seashells spit from the Atlantic to bleach on the sandy shore in the gentle caress of warm sunshine. There had been a storm the previous night and that morning, and the ocean clung to the remnants and the waves rose high and crashed to the shore with gusto.

I approached unnoticed, following my dad's gaze out to the sea, wondering what was captured in his crinkled, squinting eyes. The object of his attention was not the ship on the horizon or the gulls soaring on the wind and bobbing on the gray water, but rather, a large battered conch shell rolling in the underbelly of the rising waves. With each pulling back of the swells, it showed itself, teasing Dad and beckoning him to venture into the surf.

He smiled at me.

I said, "You've got to be kidding."

It was only a second. For a mere second, I turned my head toward a squawking gull, and when I turned back he was gone from my side, running like a peg-legged pirate straight into the solid face of the wave, which was slowly beginning to break high above his head. I ran, and as I reached him, he bent to pluck the shell. I grabbed his left arm, pulled him upright, and ran back toward the safety of the beach, where my husband was now standing frozen in awe at our stupidity.

Arm in arm, Dad with his precious conch and me with my precious Dad, we pressed on toward shore. But we were not fast enough. The towering wave curled above our heads, and then everything went green as we were cut down, so near safety. When the water pulled away, we were on our knees, as if in prayer, our hair plastered to our heads and eyeglasses pushed to the ends of our noses. As we knelt there for a moment, attempting to gather some composure, I looked at Dad, who had little bits of seaweed and stuff dangling from his unshaven chin whiskers, and I noticed that, astonishingly, he was still in possession of his prize. The conch shell was clutched to his chest by his strong and healthy right hand.

Dripping and bedraggled, we plodded back to the condo in our spongy shoes to find Mom just easing out of a deep Miami sleep. She was thankful my husband and I were there, as it enabled her to sleep to a more civilized hour. It seemed the ocean air invigorated Dad, prompting him to rise at the break of first light each morning. He had found a small grocery store and delicatessen around the corner that sold giant economy-sized cellophane bags of cheap orange cheesies, which he brought back to the condo to feed the clamorous seagulls at the unreasonably early hour of 6:00 every morning. When the commotion had successfully awakened most of the tenants in the complex, he would drag a few deck chairs from the beach to the porch just beneath the bedroom window to entertain his new friends, making sure they spoke up so Mom could hear all the local gossip from the comfort of her bed.

Dad passed away peacefully in 1991, and his old conch shell is still on the mantel where he left it.

I once told Mom that sometimes, when I miss my Dad the most, I purchase a bag of French fries or cheap orange cheesies and take them to the mall parking lot in the early morning to feed the gulls.

She said, "You've got to be kidding."

And I said, "No."

—*Marie Schnerch*

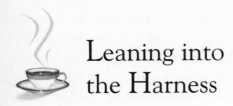

Leaning into the Harness

Her name doesn't follow "I love you" in a greeting card very often. When it does, it's an occasion. But if you look closely, her signature is written in the stoop of her tired shoulders, in the deep creases worn into her brown face by silent smiles and unspoken worries. Her signature isn't often written for her children; her signature is her children.

She is mother to eight, all grown. Some live near her, others are at a distance. Yet geography has less to do with closeness than one might think, and intimacy isn't dictated by a span of miles.

She has always been practical, always gotten things done. Over the years, she has spent more time flattening tortillas than tying bows into her daughters' hair. But there was a double portion of love pressed into those tortillas.

Through divorce, death, alcoholic husbands, and

too much hardship, she set one foot in front of the other and met the basic needs of her children. They were fed, clothed, housed, and loved. But there were no frills.

She is a woman who has lived her life as a workhorse, and when there was an added need to be met, she leaned into the harness just a little bit harder. At the age of seventy-two, that part of her nature hasn't changed. Not one bit.

Indeed, she looks for the needs that must be met, and she does what she must do to meet them. She goes to work at the Riverside Wal-Mart as a greeter and works her shift in pain. She has lupus, arthritis, hearing loss, and glaucoma, in addition to the expected aches and pains of any woman her age. She is recovering from a bleeding ulcer, and when she was too weak to return to work standing, she returned in a wheelchair.

Why? Because there was a need. And as has so often been the case, it wasn't her need, but someone else's.

Her youngest son and his family needed help making ends meet, and she just doesn't have it in her to give any less than her best. She wastes no time on laying blame for the lack of income and instead invests herself in filling the gap.

But the price is her time, and there never has been enough to go around.

For each child's tear that she wiped away,

another slipped down a cheek beyond her reach. For each sorrow she helps her children and grandchildren endure, there is another that she knows nothing of. And no price can be put on those unconsoled tears and unrelieved sorrows.

But she is human, she is finite, and she is doing the best she can.

As her life continues to unfold, she invests each day. She resolutely sets her face toward the goal of helping those who struggle, those with obvious needs.

Some of her grown children feel shortchanged and often rightly so. People with successful personal lives and careers don't need their mother less. Yet, it must be remembered that this woman's life is an elaborate weave of hardship and modest victories. And there are secrets in her fabric. There are reasons she is burdened by the needs of those who flounder.

Maybe she still wakes up at night and remembers what childhood was like after her own mother died. Her well-intentioned father took his children to live with his sister while he traveled on a railroad job. It took all his savings to buy them a decent bed to sleep in, and then he tearfully said good-bye.

Before he was out of the city limits, that bed was taken over by another relative, and the kids were introduced to the cold clay floor. They slept every night on the hard-packed earth with a dirty quilt to keep them warm—except when their father came to visit.

Her life has never been about accumulating possessions for herself. It has been, and still is, about making sure her children and grandchildren don't have to do without the basic comforts of life. Over the years, her routine of necessity has become her routine of happiness. Leaning into the harness is the equivalent of being needed; it is what she does best. Yes, tears are shed that she knows nothing about. And yes, she sheds private tears of her own.

Hers is the kindly brown face in a California Wal-Mart. She doesn't often sign greeting cards, but her signature appears like clockwork on the back of the small paycheck she shares. In her own way, she will always stand between her children and the harshness of a cold clay bed.

Hers is a practical, unassuming courage—and for one small family, it makes all the difference.

—*Christy A. Caballero*

This View

First, there were cockroaches climbing up my legs in the shower. Next, the refrigerator broke and the landlord told me she should never have given us one in the first place. Then, after unpacking the kitchen boxes and completing our first trip to the grocery store, I returned to find our porch windows removed, with the same landlord hanging out of them, yelling at me for being afraid that, yes, someone might break in while she waits a couple of days to fix them. This is the view that greeted me in a charming old apartment in a desirable section of Los Angeles.

Two weeks into our new city I let the words out. I explained to my six-year-old daughter that maybe it would be better to go back to our hometown of Atlanta, get an affordable house, a puppy, a working refrigerator. Backlit by the watercolor flowers she'd painted on our first day and that I'd promptly thumb-tacked to the wall to mask the bareness, she landed her eyes on me. In a glance I could see that she missed the cozy apartment we'd just left in Portland, she missed her old school and her young friends, she even missed the rain. But mostly she missed the mommy who, up until three months ago when I'd first contemplated moving to this outrageously expensive city, was calm enough to snuggle with her on the couch and eat popcorn and watch movies.

Still, she said, "But we just got here!" And I knew she was right.

A few haggard weeks later, after receiving legal papers from my ex-husband, I dragged myself to meet with a lawyer. After discussing my options, I con-fessed to him that I didn't know whether I could make it in this fast, expensive, noisy city, let alone manage another legal battle. He looked at the stack of court documents on his desk from our first move to Portland. Then he looked at me.

"This is the work of a woman who wants her independence," he said. "Now you have it, so don't wait for a man or anyone else. Do what you need to do to be self-sufficient."

Yes, but how? I thought as I looked past his dark antiques and out his massive windows framing a view that lifted high above all the noise and straight to the heart of a quiet mountain. *I want to write. I want to take care of my daughter. And I don't want a nine-to-five job to take me away from either.*

"What are you going to do back in Atlanta?" He paused to picture it. So did I, but before I could speak, he said, "So many writers come to this town to sell screenplays, and many do. Why can't you be one of those people?"

I felt lifted up under his confident gaze and actually began to wonder, *Why not me?* That is, after all, why we moved to L.A. Because, besides wanting to live in the sunshine after years in the Pacific Northwest rain, I wanted to explore another area of writing, take on the challenge of another mountain, and my first screenplay had drawn the interest of a producer.

When I left the lawyer's air-conditioned office tower and met my mother outside on the hot, busy street, I told her I was going to stay. She had come to visit me, or rescue me, but after hearing my announcement, we went straight back to my apartment so she and my daughter could make a year's supply of matzo balls and I could do some work. Later she helped me clean and organize my closets. They looked so beautiful when she was done, I quietly prayed I would find the courage to stay and enjoy them and not disappoint her, or my daughter, or the lawyer who'd taken the time to speak to me like a father, or myself.

After I found the rhythm of my new computer keys and the rejection letters began to trickle back in while my painfully high rent check went out, I received a rare phone call from my own father. He wasn't a talker before he got sick, but since he became ill, months passed without my hearing his voice. He told me that he and my mother were going to visit my great aunt in Canada, because she suddenly got very weak.

"There's nothing wrong," he said. "She's just tired of living and gave up the fight."

Those words hung in the precious pause between us, because they came from a man who watched his powerful, six-foot-tall frame shrink closer and closer to a piece of wood. Daily, he struggles with Parkinson's disease—to turn over in bed, to get up from a chair, to eat without choking, to walk without falling, even to talk. So his words come slowly, with difficulty, lodging somewhere midstream, long after leaving his razor-sharp mind.

"You have to decide to stay in the fight," my father continued, "because life is a battle. You can't give up."

Once again, in talking about someone else, he illuminated something about himself. The self who took a little boy with a fourth-grade education away from his Canadian home and eventually to America to become a multiple patent holder and a leader in the textile engineering field. The self who had little patience for a shy, artistic daughter and so barraged her with adages about toughness and always taking the next business-wise step. The self who accepted a life of stillness after his body forced him to give up running through the thousands of square feet of his beloved factory, creating thunderous machines as fast as his mind could imagine them.

Now, he spends his days by a tree-filled window, sitting at the kitchen table I grew up at, reading bright catalogs with a magnifying glass, watching the birds come to their feeder, and listening to and advising his six children, who fly back and away, again and again.

Every day he gets out of bed, with help, and he still travels, with help. And he talks when he can. If I get him on the phone when I call, he asks all about my progress, and when I tell him I published another piece, he tells me he believes in each step I take. Because his voice, like his body, has been weakened, he delivers his words gently, slowly, softly. So, now, I can hear them.

When I ask what he is doing, he tells me about the wonderful blue sky or about sitting by a warm fire during a hard rain, and I drink in his wisdom of acceptance, the gift to his continuing peace in life. And I like the man he has become.

Months later, with most of our boxes finally unpacked, my windows and refrigerator fixed, and even more of my daughter's flowering pictures on the walls, we have settled into a routine. Every Sunday, I set weekly writing goals, and every Friday, if I meet them, I reward myself with a latté and a cinnamon twist from Starbucks, and I always save half of the pastry for my daughter. So when I come to pick her up from camp, she knows whether it's been a good writing week or a bad one.

I have also taken up running, something I gave up years ago in the wet, gloomy darkness of Portland. But I don't run because it's sunny here almost every day, and I don't run because there are more perfect bodies in Los Angeles than I have ever seen in my life. I run because I can.

And I run because, as my feet meet the sidewalk, I digest my life changes and discover new lines for my stories, and as the palm trees tickle my peripheral vision, I dream.

And I run because as I count down the blocks in descending order—eighteen, seventeen, sixteen—I know when my feet land on block one, my eyes will be rewarded with the most humbling stretch of the Pacific Ocean. Some days I stand on the path above the beach, taking in the endless kingdom of liquid blue. Some days I run down the slope and over the bridge onto the sand, to smell the water and listen to the waves moving toward and away from the land.

Then, I remind myself to stay in the fight, while I surrender to this view.

—Lisa J. Solomon

Eva: Princess of True Grit

I retreated to the sanctuary of my bedroom, where I stayed for more than two weeks, coming out only to eat and bathe. Miserable, consumed with grief, I would have gladly stayed in there forever. But my mother was unsympathetic.

"Enough is enough, Beth. Pull yourself together and get back to school. You are going to fail. Now, get dressed, wash your face, and get to school."

"I don't care. I am not ready," I pleaded.

Ignoring my pleas, she picked up my jeans from the floor, tossed them in my face, and slammed my bedroom door behind her. The degree of the door slam indicated her mood. This slam was off the Richter scale. I knew she was serious.

I glanced at my reflection in the mirror and was horrified at the swollen, puffy-eyed mongrel staring back at me. The girl who thought of herself as one of the prettiest girls in school no longer existed.

Mom would just have to understand, I needed one more day. No way was I leaving the house looking like that. I bargained with Mom, and she conceded. She even helped me by slicing cucumbers for me to place over my eyes, to help reduce the puffiness.

The next day I borrowed my mother's hunk-of-junk car and drove to school. I thought of all the wonderful memories Princess and I'd shared together, and had to stifle my tears. I parked all the way at the far end of the lot, hoping nobody I knew would see me. When I got to my sociology class, I was greeted with sympathetic faces—and also not-so-sympathetic ones. It was Sharon's snickering that got me thrown out of class that day. Sharon was my high school nemesis. And as luck would have it, we'd not only ended up at the same community college, but also in the same class. The truth was, Sharon was the prettier of the two of us, but she wasn't very nice. Sharon had seen me parking my mom's car that morning and she could not resist laughing at me.

"Nothing like adding a little insult to injury is there, Beth?" she'd sneered during the sociology lecture.

Frustrated and fed up with Sharon's sophomoric behavior, I told her off. Because I disrupted the class, my professor demanded I leave. Humiliated, I hurried out of the classroom, with Sharon's giggle following me out the door.

I ran into the women's restroom, plunked down on a toilet, and burst out crying. I hollered out loud to God, asking why he was doing this to me, that I was a decent person, that I didn't deserve this! My crying and griping continued for several minutes. Then, I heard a faint tap-tap-tap on the restroom door. I was befuddled and somewhat annoyed: Who—better yet, why—would anyone be knocking on the door of a public restroom? I grabbed some toilet paper and dabbed at my eyes. It was probably Sharon, coming to gloat. I was sick of the stupid rivalry and ready for a long overdo face-off. I jerked open the door.

It was not Sharon. In fact, I was not face-to-face with anyone. In the doorway was a young woman about my age in a wheelchair, and she was crying. I felt like I'd been slapped in the face. I stepped back as I held open the door, allowing her to roll herself into the restroom. She apologized for knocking, but said she was not strong enough to open the door. I took a quick look at the girl. One of her hands was gnarled into a deformed fist. I couldn't see her legs because of the long skirt she wore. I really didn't want to see them anyway. I wanted to get the heck out of there as fast as I could.

Between sobs, she introduced herself as Eva. She explained that her full-time aide had called in sick that day. I listened intently, worried that she was telling me, a complete stranger, about her aide. Eva said that if she missed class today, she would flunk out of school. I told her I understood, letting out a sigh of relief.

"No, I don't think you do," she said as she began to cry harder.

"Stop crying, Eva, please. I have used up all the toilet paper on my tears. We are down to our sleeves," I said, trying to ease some of the tension with levity.

She blew out an exaggerated breath, as if to release some of her anxiety. Eva explained that without the help of a caregiver, she was unable to maneuver herself onto the toilet and to use her hands and balance her body to complete the task of relieving herself.

As the realization of what she was trying to say dawned on me, I held up my palm in a say-no-more gesture. There was no need for her to further humiliate herself by verbalizing what was painfully obvious. I wheeled her into the handicapped stall, and again spoke to God, privately that time. Fearing I wasn't strong enough to lift Eva, which would only make her feel worse, I prayed for the strength to lift her from the chair. I was shocked when I cupped my arms under her legs and scooped her up like an infant; she was light as air. It was not until I'd lifted her skirt to place her on the toilet that I glimpsed the bottom half of her torso.

Eva's legs had withered away from atrophy. We worked together in silence, tears still falling from Eva's face, as we concentrated on the job at hand.

Forty-five minutes later, which felt like a lifetime, we were finished. While washing our hands, Eva broke the silence. She told me about her dreams of getting a college degree. Her family and friends had told her it was impossible for someone in her condition. She understood that they meant well and just wanted to spare her any more heartache, but she disagreed. She looked at me so intensely her eyes took on a different shape.

"It's impossible for me to ever walk again, but my brain is fine. It will just be harder. Not impossible."

To this day, I have never seen such passion or drive as I did that day in Eva's eyes. She then asked me why I had been crying. For a few seconds, I was struck dumb with shame, but when I began to tell her, she must have seen the embarrassment on my face, because this time she did the palm-up, say-no-more gesture. I wheeled Eva out of the restroom, and we said our goodbyes.

As she turned to roll away, she stopped and turned back to me. "It was a really nice car, Beth. Maybe someday you will get another one."

My mouth fell open. After a second, I was able to speak. I had never seen this girl before that day. I asked her how she new about my car.

"Are you kidding, Beth? I see you every day. You had the nicest car in the lot. It was sweet, really sweet," she said. "Take care of yourself. I'll see you around. Thanks again, for everything."

As I watched, stunned, as Eva rolled away, a warm feeling came over me, and I turned my gaze upward. "Wow! I get the message, God." I washed my puffy, mascara-streaked face and never shed another tear over my stolen brand-new gold Pontiac Firebird Trans Am with T-top and "PRINCESS" vanity plates.

I did see Eva again, on graduation day. Only one of us got her degree that day. I was glad it was Eva. Her family, friends, and I gave her a standing ovation. More than twenty years later, I have never forgotten Eva or the lesson in courage she inadvertently taught me that day.

—*Beth Rothstein Ambler*

The Eagle and the Sparrow

Certain people come into your life and an innate instinct kicks in, telling you that it was meant to be, that some divine purpose is at work. Twenty-five years ago I met such a person. From the moment our eyes met, I knew she would affect my life in a profound way.

Finding the right words to describe this friend is difficult. Inspirational? Certainly. Role model? Indeed. Beautiful? Definitely, though not only in the traditional sense—for it is her spirit that is the most magnificent to behold.

For many years this friend climbed the corporate ladder carrying the weight of many responsibilities on her shoulders. She has always believed that all things are earned through hard work, discipline, and sacrifice. So, she continued to scale the steps of adversity. But it left her feeling overwhelmed and fatigued and joyless.

As the years flew past her, the luxury of free time and a light spirit became a distant memory. Deadlines, meetings, and endless tasks became her most intimate companions. Friends, family, and coworkers alike looked on in envy at her accomplishments. Few seemed to recognize the staggering hours she put in, the sacrifices she made, the stellar work she performed. All they noticed were the big bucks, the prestige, the superficial perks. Instead of wishing my friend well, they wallowed in self-pity and coveted her achievements.

It is not surprising, then, that those same people were flabbergasted when my friend decided to trade in her hefty yearly salary, bonuses, incentives, company car, perks, and high-powered executive lifestyle for an armload of textbooks.

Ignoring everyone's objections and warnings, she stepped off the corporate ladder and into a classroom. At age forty, she entered the university, but not, as many assumed, to earn another business degree or to further advance her business career. To the bewilderment of her critics, she "threw away" a lucrative career to become a teacher.

Indifferent to the criticisms and undaunted by the challenges, my friend succeeded in earning a master's degree and a teaching certificate. I can only imagine how daunting an undertaking it must have been.

At the graduation ceremony, bedecked in the traditional cap and gown, she strode gracefully across the stage to accept her diploma, a soft smile on her face. I stood and clapped loudly, shouting, "Bravo, bravo!"

As I watched her leave the platform, holding her teaching certificate firmly between slender fingers, I realized that she had been my teacher for the past twenty-five years. From her example I had learned how to laugh and how to dream. I'd learned the difference between growing old and growing as a human being. I'd learned that regret is a useless and avoidable condition, and that the greatest regrets are not for the things we've done, but for the things we haven't done. She has modeled the fine art of letting go of the past and of letting your life light shine today, illuminating the path to your future.

The graduation ceremony was followed by a dinner party in her honor at a local restaurant. I arrived to find a crowd of guests already in line to wish her well. When I reached her, she whispered confidentially to me that her face was numb from smiling. We laughed as old friends do, and I searched for appropriate words to say, but could find none. So I simply hugged her close, my eyes swimming with tears of pride.

Today, when I think of my friend, the newly transformed teacher, the image of a proud eagle standing on a rocky ledge, feathers ruffling in the breeze, comes to mind. A small sparrow stands directly behind the grand bird. They are fathoms apart in appearance and ability, the sparrow but a slight imitation of its magnificent cousin. The eagle spreads her massive wings and soars proudly into the sky, setting a pace the small sparrow cannot possibly hope to match. Regardless, inspired by the eagle's strength and splendor, the sparrow takes flight and follows, her heart beating rapidly.

Perhaps I will never be an eagle, but thanks to my friend, I, too, can fly.

—Beate Korchak

No More Waiting

Some years ago I worked as a waitress in downtown New York City at a popular Greenwich Village restaurant. The place is quite famous, one in which the customers buy T-shirts with the restaurant's logo on them and beg in vain for the secret recipe for its trademark house salad dressing, an item poured liberally over almost every dish on the menu.

I lived upstairs in the same building as the restaurant. This meant I could wake up ten minutes before work, brush my teeth, grab an apron, and race down just in time for my shift. It also meant that I was called upon—frequently—to fill in for absentee and tardy waiters. Now, there's nothing as irritating as sitting down with a pint of ice cream and a newly released video, and just as the opening credits roll, absentmindedly picking up the ringing telephone to hear someone shout at you (over deafeningly loud alternative rock music booming in the background), "Joy, we need you right now. Marcie's sick, and Tom's car broke down in Brooklyn. For God's sake, please come now!" Saying no during a crisis meant fewer hours and lousier shifts on the next schedule, so I tended—frequently—not to answer my phone.

Don't get me wrong: I liked my job. It was a fun and casual place to be, with young, interesting people, both those who worked there and those who came there to eat. As for the food, well, I'd been addicted to the house dressing long before I went to work there. But however much I liked the job, it was still just a job and its sole purpose was to bring in money while allowing me to maintain maximum freedom and flexible work hours.

Truth be told, I had no genuine career aspirations, in any field. After studying theater in college, my ambition for the footlights had dwindled and I felt quite content to simply enjoy life and ponder its hidden meanings. Offering customers countless refills of watery coffee and "desserts with that" provided ample job satisfaction. I was happy with my lot . . . until Valeria came.

Valeria was a fellow waitperson (or were we still waitresses back then? I can't remember when political correctness hit the food service profession). She was gorgeous and sexy and had the sweetest smile you've ever seen. But as a waitress Valeria was . . . let's just say she left plenty to be desired. With a bad case of frayed nerves along with a severe attitude problem, she was short with customers and rude to coworkers, not to mention having a chip on her shoulder the size of an aircraft carrier. Add to this the fact that she was consistently late and always jockeying to be the first to go home, and you get the picture of someone not in line to win any waitress-of-the-year awards.

So, it only goes to reason—that is, only in some warped, alternate universe—that a few years after I'd been on staff and about six months after Valeria had first set foot in the place, she was chosen to replace a day manager who was leaving.

That, of course, was not the first time I had witnessed a fellow waiter be promoted to manager; I had watched many a waiter begin that promising ascent to managerial fame and glory only to crash and burn. There was Paula, a young waitress who disappeared into rehab and then reappeared three months later as manager, only to do another disappearing act one day in the middle of lunch rush. There was Mason, the numerology guru, who seemed to have been promoted to manager in order to facilitate the sideline "dealership" he ran from the basement office. I never resented my former co-waiters in their newfound positions, and as they lorded their newly elevated status over the rest of us, I just smiled, Zen-like, at their pitiful attempts to assert their newfound authority that had been given but not really earned. I felt confident and superior in my own chosen profession of food service provider, and I envied them not, nor did I seek to change my own state of affairs. Then Valeria became manager.

Valeria in power was a thing to behold, creating in all of us the belief that nightmares really do come true. She barked orders and insults at the staff, treating us as if we were a subsector of humanity. She looked for things to criticize, watching for people to make mistakes, so that she could swoop down on them like a bird of prey before going down to the office to have a panic attack. The whole situation was ridiculous; it was way more than I could handle and maintain my serenity, and something inside me snapped. Unbidden, unexpected, unforeseen, from the depths of my soul and born fully grown like Pegasus out of Medusa's neck, came the thought that I would become a manager. Lava-like, the raging torrent of desire burst from within me, and to my utter shock it came accompanied by a bone-chilling, heart-stopping, brain-crunching, and completely unexpected emotion: abject fear.

For years I had criticized every manager who had set foot inside the restaurant. I had filled myself with an ever-growing, self-righteous indignation that in their place I could have done much better. Now, I was face to face with the fact that my motivation for staying a waitress all those years might not have been as pure as I'd imagined and might, in fact, have been based on the belief that I didn't have what it took to handle responsibility, handle a business, handle employees.

My past flashed before me, and I could see the aborted attempts and discarded ideas. No wonder I'd so seldom failed: I'd so seldom tried. Shocked into self awareness, and before the god Hypnos could lull me back to sleep and push all of those revelations back down into my subconscious, I decided to break from my history and prove that I could succeed and . . . well, manage.

I stayed awake that whole night composing a letter to the owner, trying to project all the qualities one might look for in a manager within two short typewritten paragraphs. The next morning, bags under my eyes but wired with anticipation, I sent the letter off to the head office.

The next month was an excruciating, nonstop roller-coaster ride of emotion as fears, doubts, and worries. Then, just as I started thinking that maybe I'd been foolish to think anyone could possibly want me to be in charge of anything, management announced that Valeria was leaving and they were searching for a replacement. A spark of hope danced within, and I waited anxiously to hear whether I was being considered for the position.

Only one other person, a sympathetic fellow

named Ray who had somehow transcended natural law to become both a manager and a human being, knew of my application for manager. In the event of failure, I didn't want to be pitied or scorned, so I nursed my hope and fear in silence, longing desperately for the job I now could practically taste. I knew that if I were passed over and the job went to someone else, I'd have to quit. I'd gone through some kind of gate, and whatever the outcome, could never go back. So, there I stood, trembling in the wings, waiting for the curtain to rise, not knowing whether I'd get my cue to come on out or whether I would remain a mere understudy to someone else's stardom.

Finally, one Tuesday morning in the middle of a shift, Ray came over and told me, "Wes is here, at the bar. Can you go talk with him?" Wes was the owner's number-one guy, the person who oversaw all the owner's restaurants and was involved in all high-level administrative decisions. Was this my big interview? Had my chance finally come? My heart did somersaults and flips, and my face flushed red and then white (or maybe white and then red). It had to be good news, it had to be; otherwise, why would he even bother speaking to me? But what if it wasn't, what if . . .? Knees shaking and stomach cramping, I made my way to the bar and sat on a stool next to Wes, with whom I'd never exchanged two words.

"Hi, Joy. I'm Wes." He reached out a cold, moist

hand and momentarily squeezed mine. "Joy, we'd like to offer you a position here as manager."

Until the end of my days, I'll never forget how that sounded, how it made me feel. Neither selling my first article nor publishing my first story gave me a bigger thrill than I felt in that moment. For the first time ever, I had mustered enough belief in my own potential to risk rejection and failure. And I had won.

I hardly remember what he, or I, said after that. When asked how soon before I could start my new job, I think I whipped off my apron and set it on fire in response. And I seem to recall that after Wes left, I bounced, I skipped—heck, I flew on my new managerial wings—over to tell my coworkers the glorious news.

My new life had begun—new not just because of the new position, but also because of a newfound self-respect. The seeds of confidence had been sown and in time they would grow to see me though many difficult situations and to help me achieve some of my biggest dreams. I managed that restaurant and others within the company for many years before moving on to other callings in life. When I finally left, I took with me all that I had won, best of which was the courage to look my fears and self-doubts right in the face, and to brush them aside and reach for the stars.

—Joy Pincus

The Green Chalk Heart

Darnel had been crying since story time. No one could figure out why, but his kindergarten teacher needed to take the class to the yard for recess and no amount of effort could move Darnel from the rug. When I answered the intercom call for help, I found Darnel with his head down and the tears still running off his cheeks, making little puddles on the rug in front of him. The teacher had expressed concern about Darnel before. His family situation was difficult.

As the school psychologist, I am supposed to be able to fix such things. While the teacher took the others to the playground, I talked to Darnel. Never lifting his head, he answered my questions through his sniffles. The story his teacher had just read was a little sad, but Darnel said there was no connection between his own sadness and the story. So, I tried to offer the comfort of my presence, if not my insights, and simply chatted with him. I learned about his siblings, his friends, and his pets. The source of the tear attack would remain a mystery to Darnel and to me.

Darnel finally agreed to walk with me to the playyard next to the classroom. He stood very close by my side, motionless. Children played all around him in their own egocentric joy. Darnel remained very still, head down.

One little boy was drawing nearby with sidewalk chalk. I looked over at his work. It took me a minute to realize what it was. There at Darnel's feet was a big green chalk heart. As I studied it, the artist looked up and caught my eye. I pointed to the heart, and he responded casually, "I made it for him," and pointed to Darnel. I knew that. I just couldn't believe it. Darnel's tears had stopped and mine were on their way.

Children can be impulsive, self-absorbed little creatures. They are often naughty and clueless. But sometimes their capacity for a kind impulse is so wonderful that it's worth remembering.

As he walked back into class I asked the young artist his name.

"My name is Kevin," he said.

"I want to know your name, because I want to remember you," I said.

He smiled shyly and took Darnel's hand. Darnel went with him, head still down.

I keep an informal list of little heroes. In my work with children I often refer to them as examples of the power children have to help each other. They are also reminders of why I love my work. I have added Kevin to my list.

In training teachers on various social education programs, I suggest that they collect and share such stories with their students. Sharing with students the empowering stories of other real children helps them to see their own positive power. They also like to know that someday their stories may be shared.

Children like to hear the story of Darnel and Kevin. They can see themselves in that caring role.

They also like to hear the story about Fina, a first grader who took the time to mentor another little girl who was a new arrival from Asia and spoke no English. In third grade and in perfect English, the girl told the class how Fina had changed her life, how Fina had stuck beside her that year and helped her with everything.

Students like to hear how Victor stood up for his second-grade classmate Brian. When a boy taunted Brian, telling him, "Nobody likes you," Victor stepped forward quietly and said, "I do."

They like to hear about Des, a first grader who was always willing to sit next to a disabled classmate, who leaned on Des all the time.

These are my little heroes. In reaching beyond

their comfort zones to help others, these children encourage not only their peers, but also the adults in their lives, to open their hearts and lend a hand . . . even when doing so feels awkward or scary.

—*Susan DeMersseman*

Dad's Belt

Of all the things my dad left me when he died, a piece of an old combine belt was the most valuable. It was the belt his father had used to beat him with, and it always hung over the door to our bathroom as a reminder of how things had been but would never be again.

My father grew up poor in the remote Canadian province of New Brunswick. He worked the coal mines from an early age, and his young life was filled with hardship, hard work, and harsh discipline. The man he called his father was actually his stepfather, but he wasn't told of this fact until after the brutal man had died.

Throughout his youth, the daily routine of work and turmoil was broken only by visits from his Uncle Buck from Winnipeg. Buck was a large bear of a man, who came twice a year, like clockwork, to visit his sister and her children. My dad said he was the kindest man he'd ever met, and I guess it was his influence on my father that helped him break the cycle of abuse and forbid it from entering his own home when he became a husband and father.

We couldn't have asked for a kinder, gentler man than my dad, and we all trusted and loved him deeply. When he talked of his childhood and the beatings he'd received, his eyes would slowly slide over to the belt hanging on the wall and his whole demeanor would change. The power of those beatings must have been terrible. After these stories, I always went to bed with a heavy heart, thinking of the childhood that had been robbed from this kind and loving man.

My father taught us that no matter what happened in our lives, we would always be welcome home anytime. And we knew that we could always count on a smile and a tender word of advice to soothe us when we got there.

Time continued her dance, and we all grew up and moved out. Still, we continued to receive guidance and love from our father until the day he died. It hit us all hard. As we gathered on the old farm, tears flowed freely for this man who'd had a miserable childhood but had filled ours with affection and beauty.

In the days immediately after my father's memorial service, the lawyers came and the last wishes were stated and passed on. Although the estate was meager, we all received one gift beyond value and explanation.

In his last days, our father had taken the belt down from the wall and cut it into four pieces. We all received a piece of the belt that had hurt our father so terribly. That night, we sat around crying and discussing what he could have been thinking when he did this. As the night wore on, it began to dawn on us.

The belt symbolized everything he'd taught us not to be.

It was his trophy. He had lived through the abuse. Instead of abandoning life, like so many others might have, he'd embraced it, and in so doing, he'd turned a legacy of hate and hurt into a legacy of love and happiness.

Now, I keep that belt on my wall. We all do. It hangs as a reminder of the obstacles we can all overcome, with grace and kindness. And when my daughter is crying because she's lost her Pokémon cards or skinned her knee, I hold her close, look at that old belt, and think of a man she will never know. A man I am honored to call Dad.

—*John Gaudet*

The Rose of Tucumcari

"Walter, you're such a puritan!" It was a familiar refrain when Aunt Lula came to our house on one of her rare visits from Oregon. She was my father's older sister, third-born in a family of eleven. And as surely as she called my father puritanical, he reproached her for being "wild."

She was never on good terms with her younger siblings. Perhaps it was because she took care of them when they were small. A stern disciplinarian, she became a surrogate mother to eight younger brothers and sisters when she was only twelve. Perhaps she resented the burden, the noisy children who kept her from her reading. She had an insatiable appetite for dime novels, loved to read about pure maidens who transformed whole towns and entire tribes of wild Indians with their gentle presence.

Certainly, she was the unconventional one in a

family of somber Scots-Irish Cherokees. After I was older and had read Cherokee history, I thought Lula might be a throwback to Nancy Ward, the Pocahontas of our Cherokee people. But then, Cherokee women in general tended to be more free-spirited than Anglo-Saxon women.

Lula married the love of her life when she was twenty, and they had two beautiful daughters. It seemed she would live happily ever after, like the heroines in her dime novels. But tragedy struck swiftly and without mercy. First her young husband and then her older daughter died from tuberculosis. Anguished and destitute, Aunt Lula took her surviving daughter to California to seek their fortune. Eventually they moved to the Oregon mountains. She worked at a series of jobs, homesteaded a piece of land, scrimped and saved—and married three more times. In a time and place where divorce was rare, she divorced husbands two and three and outlived the fourth.

We rarely saw her during those years. Struggling to save our hardscrabble farms during the Depression, we had no money or time for travel. During all my years at home, Aunt Lula rode the bus to see us just three times. Her "West Coast ways" did not endear her to our remote community at Wild Horse Creek. I remember, for example, the day she mowed my grandmother Thompson's yard wearing modest

Bermuda shorts. This was in 1940, and our women were only recently out of long dresses. Bermuda shorts would not come to our section of southern Oklahoma for at least a decade. That hot August morning, I found my grandmother weeping, apron over her head.

"Grandma, what's wrong? Are you sick? Did Lula hurt your feelings?" Grandmother's Wesleyan Methodist views had clashed with Lula's modernism on more than one occasion.

"No, child, but if Mr. Williams sees Lula Mae in those shorts, with that 'split case' bonnet on her head, he'll think it's me." Amos Williams had been our rural mail carrier for as long as I could remember. A staid Southern Baptist, he was our main link to the world outside Wild Horse.

Grandma need not have worried. My extroverted aunt threw her bonnet aside and went to meet Mr. Williams when he stopped at our corner. They talked about the war in Europe while old Amos tried valiantly not to look at Lula's knees. Grandma was mortified that he should see her daughter so immodestly attired. She knew the news would travel faster than the trickle of water in Wild Horse Creek.

Aunt Lula tangled with my father, too, on that trip. They argued about politics. Lula adored Franklin Delano Roosevelt. They argued about the site of the old home place.

"It was right down there by Wild Horse Creek, Lula." My father was certain his memories were accurate.

"Walter, you're crack brained; it was there on that little rise by the road." When Lula argued with her brother, Mama and I ran for cover or hunkered down and waited "for these calamities to be over past."

After Pearl Harbor, Lula went to work in a Defense factory and made good money for the first time in her life. She married a returning veteran who turned out to be a mental case and chased her around their mountain cabin with an ax. She leaped into his rickety old pickup, having never driven a car, and drove it helter-skelter down the mountain, crashing into a filling station pump and setting the place on fire. She recounted that tragic episode on her next visit to Wild Horse. A born raconteur, she had us all laughing at her adventures—everyone except my poker-faced father and grandmother.

She had some perverse streak in her that loved to shock those two, yet she was always wounded when they criticized her.

"I can't help it if men pursue me," she told my outraged father. "After all, I have million-dollar legs." She held out those long, lithe limbs for our inspection and laughed scornfully as my father stomped out of the room.

But it was her visit in 1948 that finally estranged

her from our family. We had built a new house across from Wild Horse School. After two aborted attempts to find water on our sandstone hill, we reconciled ourselves to carrying buckets from the schoolhouse pump. Every ounce of water we used, for cooking, bathing, mopping the floor, had to be carried the half mile from the pump. In winter, the water runs were painfully cold, and in Oklahoma's August heat, sheer misery.

Aunt Lula watched us in sympathetic silence and then turned to my father.

"Walter, I can find water for you if you want to dig a well."

"Yeah, I'll bet you can." It was the sarcastic tone he frequently used with Lula.

"No, really, let's go down to the stock tank and cut some willow branches."

"Oh, no, you don't, Lula Mae Thompson. I'll not have you water-witching on my place."

"Call it what you want. I call it dowsing, and better folks than you and I have done it."

I learned later that dowsing tools had been found in King Tut's tomb. And woodcuts show that dowsing was done in China at least two thousand years before Christ. It was not until the Middle Ages that Europeans labeled dowsers "witches." Then, Martin Luther declared dowsing to be "the work of the devil." But throughout the ages and most of the world, dowsing has been considered a sixth sense that early humans needed to find the water that was essential to surviving a very hostile environment. Some believe it is a normal, sensory perception like those used by birds, fish, and animals. Hummingbirds, for example, find their way to and from Venezuela each year. Salmon use it to return to the waters of their birth to spawn. Lost dogs and cats make "incredible journeys" to return home.

Aunt Lula tried in vain to convince my father of the validity of dowsing. He snorted in disgust and went after the cows. So, she cut her willow "wand" and began to watch it intently as she stomped around our yard, the garden, and even through the house. The first "sighting" she had was in the middle of our living room. The second was a milder "dip" out under the oak tree that held my swing. She marked the spot, made her report, and packed for her return trip to Oregon. There was pained silence on the way into the bus station.

She only spoke once: "Walter, I don't care what you think of me, but surely you would not condemn your wife and this child to carrying water the rest of their days. What would it hurt for you to dig a well under the oak tree?"

My father never said a word. Grimly, he carried her cardboard suitcase out to the bus. She hugged me and turned to touch his face gently with her hand. He winced as if she had burned him.

We never saw her again.

We carried water throughout that summer and the coldest Oklahoma winter on record. In April, I came home from school one day to find my father with a shovel and a posthole digger, digging under the oak tree. He hired a crew to finish the job, and they found a gushing well of cold, clear water at sixty feet. We used it to install indoor plumbing when I was eighteen, and Mother and I blessed Aunt Lula every time we turned on the faucet or flushed the commode.

The years passed and we got word that she had buried her fourth husband and then that she had died in Oregon. Her daughter took her body to Tucumcari, New Mexico, for burial.

Two years later, when we knew my father was dying, I took him to see Colorado's lofty mountains. He had always longed to see the "mountings," and I thought an escape from Oklahoma's summer heat might give him a respite and prolong his life. We stayed three days in a cabin overlooking the mountains. It was so cool at night we needed blankets. My father, loyal Okie though he was, said he wondered why folks ever settled the dry, barren plains when Colorado was just ahead.

On our last evening, we sat watching the sunset over the mountains and breathing fresh mountain air. My father had long since come to terms with his mortality, but he knew I had not.

In the glorious silence of that sunset, he placed a gnarled hand on mine, and said, "Honey, do you remember when you was small and you would fall asleep at your grandparents' house? I'd carry you home to your own bed and next morning you always wondered, 'How did I get back to my own place?' Well, I think dying is like that: You fall asleep here and wake up in your Own Place."

He waited a minute for some response, but I could think of nothing to say. After a moment, he gazed reflectively out at the mountains and said, "I never knew till now why Lula loved the mountings so much." Then he added tentatively, "Do you think maybe we could drive back through Tucumcari tomorrow?"

I remembered Aunt Lula was buried there, but thought it strange he should want to drive out of our way to visit her grave. Nonetheless, the next day, we drove down out of the mountains and across the high plains to Tucumcari. The small cemetery was isolated, but well kept. The sexton had to show us Lula's grave, for there was no marker, just a small indentation in the barren ground.

My father was stricken. He stared at the grave site for a long while, tears dripping off his chin. "She deserves better than this; she was a hard worker." It was his highest accolade.

His next words shocked me. "She was the most

courageous woman I've ever known . . . and she really did have nice legs."

He went to the cemetery office before I could think of anything to say.

Not long before he died, he received a picture of the tombstone he had bought for Aunt Lula. I don't know if he had forgotten her four marriages or simply wanted to reclaim her for his family, but he used her maiden name:

Lula Mae Thompson
1899–1972
Judge not, that ye be not judged.

We carried one other thing away from the cemetery in Tucumcari: A small egg had rolled from its nest and lay in the depression that was my aunt's grave. I placed it in a velvet pouch that had held my turquoise bracelet, tied it to a leather thong, and wore it down inside my T-shirt for warmth. Once home, we retrieved a small incubator from the attic and hatched a Gambel's quail.

In the remaining weeks of his life, my father watched the tiny bird with amusement and affection. She was so inquisitive, so quick, and so mischievous, that, of course, he called her Lula.

—Kathryn Presley

Go, Lu, Go!

I knew I wouldn't win. From my warm-up stretch and my first deep breath before running the Fiesta Bowl ten-kilometer race, I knew I would not take home first place—would not take any prize. The honors would go to others; they always did. Not even in my physical prime, twenty or so years earlier, would I have been a contender.

In my daydreams, though, I ran like Flo Jo (Olympic gold-medalist Florence Griffith-Joyner). I often envisioned the strong muscles flexing and pumping beneath my skin, the feel of track giving beneath my feet in slow motion. I could see the finish ribbon stretched across my chest, flapping behind me as I leaned forward, arching my back, gasping for breath, smiling from ear to ear as I shook awake from my Olympian vision.

As a child, I ran everywhere. I was skinny then.

I ran across the street to my friend's house, never knocking, just shouting "Elaine!" from the porch. I ran to McMillan Park a few blocks away from home to shinny up young birch trees until they bent and I bounced on the ground, still holding onto the branches, long before I knew of the existence of Robert Frost. A quick run to the grocery store got bread or milk, and the almost daily three-mile run to Sacred Heart Elementary School saw me in a blur. I rarely walked; it took too long. Wherever I wanted to go, I could get there quickly on my own two fleet feet.

I loved how the wind tickled through my curls, especially in the Indiana summers, when the warm, sweet air smelled like flowers and warm dirt. The sun on my face deepened the blush that running brought to my cheeks. The grin I wore never drooped. I found joy in running. Running set me free.

As I grew older, other girls began to run as fast, and then faster, than me. The Franciscan nuns at Fort Wayne's Bishop Luers High School held quasi-track meets during the girls' gym classes. As a Catholic school in the early 1960s, we had no girls' track team and were forbidden to participate in athletics with the boys.

As much as I loved to run—and did run, as fast and as hard as my legs would carry me—I could not keep up with the leaders as we circled the track. Only later in life did I realize I was blessed with short, stubby legs, not exactly built for running fast. The girls with longer legs always beat me.

In the late 1980s, after my three children, who had put a halt to my running days (at least for fun, rather than after them), had become teenagers, I rediscovered my joy of running. Jogging was by then a popular pastime, and I, like many of my suburban neighbors, joined the throng. I jogged the dirt roadway along the irrigation canal behind our house in Mesa, Arizona, working up to three miles a day and shaving my time to thirty-two minutes.

I enjoyed my daily jogging. It got me outside and moving, and it gave me some rare time alone. But as time went on, curiosity gnawed at me. *Could I run a race?* At least one 10K is held in the Phoenix area each week. I was forty-three, and my running dream dangled in front of me like a carrot (or rather, like chocolate, my reward food of choice).

So, there I was on that gray dawn of New Year's Day 1990, on a road near Encanto Park in Phoenix, stretching and warming up with 500 other Nike-clad comrades. The reality of my lack of running prowess stared at me from their strong, calm faces. Their shoes bore the scars of many races. Their bodies showed the results of rigorous training. They were prepared and ready to rumble. All had been in this position many times before, of that I was certain. *What was I doing? What was I thinking, running my first*

10K race at my age, with my body, my short legs, and with my comparatively meager experience?

The starting shot rang out and a human wave dragged me along in its current. Heads popped up and down like popcorn in a skillet as several runners struggled to break free of the still barely moving mob and to reach their jogging stride. By the time the crowd thinned, enabling us to finally edge into a lope, I was already fighting for breath. The air seemed heavy with humidity and pollution and difficult to inhale.

Three miles into the race, as we rounded the corner and opened up onto Central Avenue, my lungs were searching desperately for air. My chest hurt. My muscles burned. My legs felt heavy as iron. The front-runners were far out of sight—long gone.

An older man jogging next to me noticed my struggle and said I could walk if I wanted. No. I couldn't. Not with thousands of spectators lining both sides of the road, gathered for the Fiesta Bowl Parade that would begin after the race, in less than an hour, watching as we passed. The expectant faces of those strangers pushed me forward and around the curve marking the last stretch of the race.

Forcing one foot in front of the other, again and again, I neared Encanto Boulevard and, nearly spent, crossed into the coliseum parking lot. A few yards ahead, I saw the word "Finish" above the runners in front of me. As in the daydreams of my youth, I seemed to cross the finish line, a painted stripe under the archway, in slow motion. But there was no ribbon to break. The winner had broken through it thirty-three minutes earlier—in half my time of sixty-six minutes.

I slowed my stride to a walk and finally stopped, put my hands on my hips, and bent forward to ease the pressure on my lungs. I hadn't won the race. I knew I wouldn't. Not even close. But I did finish the entire 10K—running, on my own two feet.

Still gasping for breath, a wide smile spread across my flushed cheeks. For a few brief moments, I was once again that joyous child, running like the wind.

—*Lu Stitt*

Ninety-Day Wonder

When I dream about my father, as I often do, he is usually teaching me something. His voice is firm, bellowing through the room like a drill sergeant with a new recruit. Sometimes, his hand flies up to gesture and I flinch, duck my head, afraid he might rap me for having let my attention wander.

A few months after my birth, in 1944, the U.S. Navy sent my father to Officer's Candidate School at Cornell University. He was among a select group of men chosen to complete the equivalent of a college education in just three months. The Navy called them "ninety-day wonders." In his mostly ordinary life, this hailed as an extraordinary achievement, and it was probably why he expected nothing less than academic excellence from his children. To my father, second best was a close cousin to failure.

Now, while visiting my parents' Florida home, I watch my father proudly show me racks of golf slacks hung meticulously and arranged by color in his closet. He lifts the bamboo shade and gestures toward the sun, gloating, as if he were responsible for it being there. It's a great day for the driving range. At last, he can hit that little white ball again. I agree, reluctantly, to let him give me a golf lesson today.

Just a year ago, the choice of what to wear seemed insignificant, almost banal, among decisions of what stocks to buy or sell or where to travel during his comfortable state of semiretirement. Then, like a flash tropical storm, his life changed dramatically. Two days after elective bypass surgery at the age of seventy-two, he suffered a massive stroke. He had decided on the surgery after several consultations and opinions, the consensus being it could add ten, maybe twenty, years to his life.

The operation was a clinical success. He said post-op that he'd felt minimal pain and discomfort. So, on the second day, he became a little stubborn, insisted on a trip to the bathroom over the indignity of using a bedpan. It may have been the mistake of his life. It caused a blood clot to travel and lodge in the left portion of his brain, the part that controls patterns of speech, communication, and the memory bank of learning. The stroke paralyzed his right side. All his words and thoughts lay trapped inside him.

I flew to Florida immediately, not knowing what to expect, shocked at the sudden change in his condition.

My mother begged me not to become emotional when I saw him. She instructed me to talk very slowly. Then she said, "The man in that room is not your father."

Those words echoed in my mind as I walked down the endless corridor to his room. He was propped in a huge vinyl chair with support bars. Twisted tubes connected him to a machine that made loud pumping sounds, like an aquarium. His left arm was bent, the hand pressed against his cheek, holding up his head. He looked 100 years old. I gulped hard, choking back tears, while I stood frozen at his right side.

"Hi, Daddy," I said, the endearment startling me; I hadn't uttered it in years.

He groaned, and I bent over to kiss him, chatting nervously, trying to avoid his sad liquid eyes. But they searched my face, looking for answers to all the questions he could not ask.

"Don't worry," I said. "Everything will be all right."

In the days that followed, doctors rotated into and out of his room, looking for hints of improvement. They did not recognize this new patient as the vibrant man who had marched into their office just weeks before, methodically gathering information, captain of his own destiny. Now, they seemed to press him too hard, asking for the names of his children and his wife. He looked at them with disgust, annoyed at this test. They dangled simple familiar objects in front of his face: a comb, a ball, a cup. When he shoved the rubber ball into his mouth, I threw myself over his chest and squeezed his cheeks until he released it. He could name nothing.

But once in utter frustration, he screamed, "Get out of here, all of you!" Involuntary speech caused by pure anger.

After further testing, the speech pathologist reported that his impairment was severe. There was a chance he could endanger himself, mistake or misuse a razor, a fork, a knife. Recovery would be an uphill battle. It would depend on his willingness to relearn the simplest of concepts and on loads of sheer luck.

Within a few days, in the same hospital, he began his rehabilitation. Although he suffered bouts of depression, he waited anxiously for his daily speech and physical therapy. He sat staring at his watch, always ready for someone, anyone, to knock on his door. *Could he really know the time*, I wondered, *or was it just habit?* Like a toddler, he struggled trying to feed himself with a spoon. He insisted on trying to walk, grunting loudly if you dared stop him. He developed a new vocabulary of four-letter words, commonplace for stroke victims. The staff cheered him on as he marched tentatively down the long hospital halls in his first pair of Nike high-tops. He responded like Rocky, with arms raised and garbled words that sounded like, "I'll do it. You'll see."

In less than three weeks, my father walked unassisted and went home. He continued speech therapy at home on a computer. He sat for hours, mesmerized by the images on the screen. The therapist used simple preschool programs designed to help him link sounds with words that suddenly appeared new, as if never learned. He was starting over.

I told his therapist he would work harder than anyone. I told her of his passion for knowledge, about the Navy and Cornell. I told her how he was constantly sending us, his children, articles to read; words of advice and concern substituted for words of love. She listened but turned from me, from my pleading eyes. She already knew what I was afraid to hear: My father was no longer the man I'd known; she would not dare forecast his future.

Dad's emotions have taken the place of much of his language. Yet, while watching him through this struggle, I am learning from him still.

His little notebook lists addresses and our names, names he might never again say. He gives out business cards describing his disability to anyone who looks at him with trepidation. Sometimes when our family gathers around the dinner table, his head darts back and forth as he desperately tries to take in the nuances of our conversation, determined to be an active participant no matter what. He laughs when we laugh, leans in when we whisper. As I watch him struggling to understand, my heart pounds and I urge everyone to please slow down. When they don't, his eyes often meet mine. "Oh, God," I might hear him whisper.

Today, I'm startled when my father walks out of his bedroom modeling lime-green golf slacks and, smiling broadly, says, "Good, huh?"

What can I possibly say to this wondrous man, who's fought far longer than ninety days to perform these simple and momentous tasks, to utter the simplest of phrases? What else, but . . .

"Perfect!"

—*Sande Boritz Berger*

Against All Odds on the Field of Dreams

Dumisane Ntombela is the miracle child of Vosloorus, a poverty-stricken township in the east of Johannesburg, South Africa. He was just two when bilateral retinoblastoma cancer struck him, completely destroying his eyes. It is difficult to say which has been harder on Dumisane: being blind or being ostracized for his disability, labeled "the ghost" and beaten up by ignorant children and superstitious neighbors.

Head hung down, this small boy quietly recalls the terror of being unable to protect himself because he couldn't see where the next punch or kick was coming from. Threats and discrimination extended to his family, and his father, Abel, was once jailed because of malicious false allegations from neighbors. Being a "criminal" cost him his job.

Having a criminal record makes work hard to

find, and Abel's loss of income, together with legal and bail fees, has financially crippled the Ntombela family. Yet, somehow, they remain optimistic, warm, and generous. Despite their daily struggle, no one who passes through their little shack goes without food, drink, and friendship.

The absence of his father during his internment was Dumisane's most difficult experience of all. He worried terribly and begged the other members of his family not to defend him from his attackers, fearing they would meet the same fate as his father if they did. During these times, he would ask his mother to wash the blood from his wounds and insisted that the Lord would help him through his trials.

Abel, in the hope that Dumisane would excel in something, taught him to play the keyboard at an early age. Who knows? Maybe his son would be the next Stevie Wonder.

But Dumisane's real passion was soccer. He yearned to join in with the other children. Most of them had no interest in playing soccer with a blind boy. Rejected over and over again, he soon realized there was only one way he'd ever be able to play soccer: He would have to start his own soccer club. He would call it the Silver Spears.

And that's exactly what he did. With considerable coaxing, he managed to find a handful of boys willing to play soccer with him. Proving that he could play despite his blindness, other boys joined his soccer club, and Dumisane's dream became a reality. The Silver Spears soon started challenging other teams—and winning.

By saving the winnings from their games, as well as his monthly disability grant from the government and contributions from his grandmother's pension, Dumisane eventually had enough money to buy his team their very own soccer ball, jerseys for the players, and boots.

No longer was Dumisane bored and lonely. Now, he had freedom, and like the other children, he ran barefoot down the dusty street to the soccer field, kicking the soccer ball back and forth to his mates. For the first time in his life, at age nine, he had friends and was happy.

But owning and managing his own soccer club is just part of Dumisane's victory. And getting there has been a long and agonizing process. His eight months of intensive chemotherapy and radiotherapy involved painful tests, lumbar punctures, and drips. Although the treatment was successful and the cancer is in remission, the fear that it may strike again is always there.

Though Dumisane cannot see the ball, the goal posts, the other players, or even the field on which he runs, he knows the game of soccer backward and forward. His family often watches it on television, especially when Dumisane's favorite team, the Orlando Pirates, is on. As the others watch the game, Dumisane listens intently to the commentators, and when asked what he "saw," he describes everything about the game.

This inner vision is also what helps Dumisane to play, and he's on the field daily, with the help of his father and older brother. With his strongly developed senses of hearing and touch, Dumisane listens carefully and feels the vibrations on the field. In this way, he establishes the location of the ball and the other players. When the ball is near him, his teammates shout and direct him to the goal post—and he scores frequently. When the game gets heated, they lead him by the hand.

Everyone who belongs to the Silver Spears must play by the rules. Not just the rules of the game, but Dumisane's rules of being kind, compassionate, and principled. Those who are nasty to others, display poor sportsmanship, or don't behave properly are asked to leave.

Soccer is not Dumisane's only ambition and achievement. He strives to be an inspiration to other disabled children, and he hopes to one day help them to join professional clubs, like the famous national team, Bafana Bafana. As a student at the Sibonile School for Visually Impaired Pupils, he learns skills that will ensure him a job, and he hopes to attend a mainstream school one day. He also wants to learn English, because he knows it will give him more opportunities than speaking only Zulu. Although he dreams of playing in the big soccer league, Dumisane also acknowledges his limitations. He plans to become a telephone operator when he grows up.

While Abel works to get his son into a mainstream school, an unexpected prospect has opened up to Dumisane that may just lead to his becoming the next Stevie Wonder after all. A film production company that heard about this miracle child wants him to star in a new television series called *Soul Buddyz—Tomorrow Is Ours*. And it surely is for this budding hero, whose inner vision and sheer determination have enabled him to break through seemingly impenetrable boundaries.

What is most extraordinary about Dumisane is that he doesn't see himself as being brave at all. He doesn't see himself as being any different from anyone else. He's just an average eleven-year-old boy who loves soccer—and sees clearly the promise in life.

—*Danya-Zee Bulkin*

The Shtick of
a Lifetime

I was standing on a stage in a blackened theater, my heart pounding. I could hear my blood throbbing in my head; everything else fell silent. My mouth went dry, and the shaking in my hands was working its way up to my shoulders. Luckily, the stage was still dark.

Then, suddenly, it wasn't. A spotlight burst through the darkness, showering my body with heat and white light. I blinked against the sharp glare, and when I opened my eyes, I was surprised to see my hands gripping the microphone in front of me. The intensity of the spotlight made the sleeves of my shirt glow funny, and I knew without a doubt that I was the most visible thing in the room. I had waited a lifetime for a moment like this. I should have felt elated. Instead, I felt only the expectant pressure of a hundred people staring at me, waiting for me to make them laugh. Now that my "big break" had arrived, all I could think about was getting it over with.

The moment had been a long time coming. I had been painfully shy as a child, from grade school all the way through high school.

Yet, beneath the shyness was a spark—a desire to perform, to entertain—glowing deep within my soul. I would watch the drama club perform in the auditorium and secretly wish I was up on stage with them. But I was always too afraid, too reserved.

In time, high school ended, and before I left for the University of Kansas, my friends and I threw a bash to celebrate the end of an era. At the party, my best friend, Mandy, pulled me aside.

"You should join your university's drama club," she told me. "You'll kick yourself forever if you don't."

"I won't have time with all my writing," I said. A lame excuse, I knew, but hiding behind my English major was easier than explaining why I was still afraid.

"Besides, the boy-to-girl ratio will be two to one," I said. "I can think of better ways to spend my free time."

Mandy laughed. "You're a funny girl," she said, then added, "Just don't get jaded when no one knows it but me."

"I've been jaded for eighteen years; why stop now?" I joked. Then, seeing the serious expression on her face, I said, "I'll think about it."

And I did, for the first week of college. When I'd finally found the courage to sign up, membership was full. Disappointed, I threw myself into schoolwork. College moved faster than high school, and it seemed like in no time at all I was in my senior year. The boy/girl ratio hadn't been quite as full of opportunity as I had first predicted, but my grades were good and the class work had kept me busy, so busy, in fact, I hadn't thought much about the stage.

Then one day, my roommate, Theresa, handed me a copy of the *Kansas City Star*, pointing to an ad she'd circled with a bright red marker. A local comedy club was having an open mic night.

"I'm not a comic," I protested.

"You're funny, and you're really into the theater," she said. "You can do this."

"Stand-up isn't theater," I said, setting the paper on my desk. "It's completely different. I wouldn't know where to begin."

"I just think you should give it a try," Theresa said, dropping the subject, but I could tell she was annoyed.

That night I called Mandy and told her about the ad and Theresa's odd behavior.

"She just sees what everyone around you has seen for a long time," said Mandy. "You belong on a stage."

I swallowed hard; my eyes were wet.

"But I'm afraid," I whispered into the phone.

"Do it anyway," she said. Then she hung up.

I was shocked. She had never hung up on me before, much less when I was on the brink of tears. I picked the ad up off my desk and tacked it to my bulletin board. The next open mic was only three weeks away. If I was going to go through with this, I had some work to do.

For the next three weeks, when I wasn't in class or studying, I was sitting in front of a word processor writing jokes, rehearsing the jokes, or watching videos of famous comedians doing stand-up routines. I would have only three minutes to perform and I wanted to give the act my best shot.

On the night before my performance, Mandy called to say she would be in town to see the act. She would meet Theresa and me at the club, and was bringing a date. I told her to tell whomever she was bringing not to expect too much. "You'll be great," she assured me.

When we hung up, I repeated her words aloud to myself: "You'll be great." But they seemed foreign and forced. Self-doubt crept in. I looked at the stack of jokes I had written, ninety-three pages worth in all, and saw mostly wasted time. It was too late to rewrite now, though. Stomach churning, I shuffled through the stack of jokes, picking out the ones I thought were the best, and jotted down key words on a note card.

The day of my performance, Theresa and I spent the afternoon figuring out what I should wear. We decided on a long-sleeved black blouse, because it showed the least amount of sweat, a red polka-dotted scarf tied around my neck for color, dark blue jeans, and a pair of black boots. A black-and-red bracelet dangled from my wrist, and a pair of long black earrings glittered on my earlobes. I looked in the mirror, satisfied: *At least I'll look the part.*

When we arrived at the club, Mandy had yet to show up. Theresa mingled, while the club owner gave me a quick rundown of when I needed to be backstage for my cue. I'd be the last to perform. *Well, I thought, that will at least give me the chance to see what the other comedians were doing—and bail, if need be.* When I rejoined Theresa, she was talking to one of the other performers.

"These crowds are rough," said the comedian. "Most of them are here to cheer on their friends, so unless the competition is really funny, they save their laughs for the people they're here to see. It's brutal."

That did it. I moved to a seat by the stage door and stayed there as the first comedian took the stage.

She was funny. Even though her jokes were mostly about cell phones, her routine went over well and the crowd was revved up. The next act was just as good, and so were the next two. Three more comedians took the stage, and as my time got closer, it was all I could do to keep myself from slipping out the back door and hanging out in the café across the street. Before I could put my escape plan into motion, though, the stage manager tapped me on the shoulder and told me to take my place backstage. I was next.

I went numb. In less than three minutes, I'd be on. I took out my card and glanced at my notes. Instantly, the jokes came to mind. I heard the audience erupt in a big laugh, and seconds later a comedian came through the stage entrance, wiping sweat from his brow.

"Good crowd tonight," he said as he passed. "Break a leg, newbie."

The stagehand nodded. I walked onto the stage. I stood under the spotlight, sweaty and terrified. I took a deep breath, and with a trembling voice began:

Good evening, Kansas City. This is my first open mic. But being an English major with a minor in philosophy, I'm used to a lot of ridicule. I'm also used to expensive school loan bills. If four years of higher education has taught me one thing, it's how to handle bills: Write a sappy poem about them and then philosophize about how they don't really exist. . . .

Big laughs. I was on a roll.

In what seemed like seconds, three minutes came and went. When it was over, I ran off stage so fast, I bumped into Mandy, who had finally shown up, just in time to hear my act. She hugged me tightly.

"I was really impressed," she said. "So was Jacob."

"Jacob?" I asked, still shaking. She pointed to where Theresa was standing, talking to a tall, handsome guy with dark hair and tiny, wire-rimmed glasses. It was Jacob Kaninsky, president of our old high-school drama club.

"Hey!" said Jacob, when he saw me. He walked over and put his arm around me. "Where were you back in high school?" he asked. "We were dying for some funny girls back then. You were awesome.

"You know," he said. "I work part time at an improv club, and I'd love to have you perform."

"Uh, of course!" I said, stumbling over the words. He handed me his number, and as I took it, a fervent heat fell over my body, even more intense than the heat of the spotlight. At first I thought I might faint, but as I put the number in my pocket, I smiled, realizing that this must be what it feels like when a life-long spark bursts into flame.

—*Amy Brady*

Darkness and Sunshine

Kirsten stands on the top of Springer Mountain, all the hardships of her journey swept away in the elation of the moment. Her mind fills with images: autumn glory in Vermont; cool lakes in Maine, reflecting starlit skies; the fragile first flush of spring, coloring late snows in Pennsylvania; the kindness of strangers; the camaraderie at hiker shelters; the gentle wit and philosophy engendered when there is time to think, entered in the trail registers.

These new memories fill the dark places created five years earlier.

It was a night of tragedy and miracles. I cannot easily forget the still, small frame of my daughter entering the maw of the CAT scanner—a cracked second vertebra in the neck, a fractured skull, no major brain damage. I threw away the turquoise silk scarf used to stanch the blood.

"It can be washed, you know," said the nurse.

I never wanted to see it again.

In the chaos after the crash, Kirsten's handbag had gone to the mortuary: Long, sterile corridors, brightly lit, cold. The other girl was taken to Johannesburg General; the guitar belonging to her was the only clue at Sandton Clinic, where Kirsten was taken. Specialists muttered, glancing in our direction. Kirsten was admitted to intensive care. Her father went home in the bleak dawn to try to find out which friend had died. Her brother, David, went to the police station to see the wrecked car and to try to find out what had happened. I sat next to my daughter through the night, knowing that when she awoke, I'd have to tell her that the friend to whom she was giving a lift was dead.

Then, a small miracle: My son strode down the long corridor, his smile like the sun. "She was on her own. The accident wasn't her fault."

Relief flooded me, only to be countered by waves of empathy for the mother of the young driver of the other car who had lost control on those black icy streets and died that night. The forlorn guitar was heartbreakingly collected by a boyfriend. The other mother and I spoke on the phone.

"At least you still have your daughter," she said.

Yes, I still had my daughter.

Her body eventually healed, but Kirsten's memory was severely impaired, first the short-term, then the long-term.

"Where am I? What happened?"

Every morning I would explain again.

"I can't remember my sister's face. I can't remember her wedding. How will I ever remember what I have studied?"

Kirsten had completed the first six months of a masters in environmental science at the University of Cape Town.

We took her home; she became our baby again. Her father delighted in reading Winnie the Pooh aloud to her. With familiar words and faces and with family and friends from various parts of the country going through photograph albums with her, slowly her body started up again. Physically, she, and we, coped. But my daughter's sunshine, her bright confidence, was gone, replaced with a haunted look in her eyes.

She completed her dissertation the following July, but the healing process was far from complete. Then Kirsten took that process out of the hands of her parents and doctors and decided on her own course of treatment. The phone rang:

"Mom, I've decided to hike the Appalachian Trail."

Our children had always been keen hikers, but this was a child recovering from a broken neck and a head injury, and the Appalachian Trail stretched for 2,100 miles.

A few weeks after we waved goodbye and Kirsten boarded her flight to New York, her letters began arriving home. Her descriptions of trail life allowed us to share her outer journey of discovery and her inner journey of rediscovery—a mixture of joy and hardship that mirrored and extended the series of events that began on that June night almost exactly a year earlier.

I dumped a whole lot of stuff in the hiker box at Abol Bridge, including my towel, several components of my medicine kit, and my favourite jeans. Finally my backpack is light enough to enable me to concentrate on things other than the pain in my neck and blistered feet.

I have done a lot of thinking about what happened, what I can and what I can't remember, and my future after the trail. But one can only do so much thinking, and by the time I reached the end of the 100-mile wilderness, I panicked about what I would think about for the next 1900 miles. Fortunately, as time passes my mind seems to have slipped into a lower gear in sync with the rhythm of my natural surroundings. I am hardly conscious of anything more than putting one foot in front of another as I journey forth.

We became familiar with the vocabulary of the trail. Kirsten was a southbound "thru-hiker" and her trail name was "Penguin Seeker." Her letters included references to "Bear Charmer," another lone female thru-hiker. The two of them decided "to look out for each other."

Most start from Georgia and arrive in Maine in the late fall. Travelling south, we have frequent encounters with northbounders. The ones that have made it as far as Maine are the hardiest of hikers, having traversed 13 states and likely to complete the entire trail in one season. Easily distinguished from day- and weekend-hikers, these guys are lean, laid back, spirited, and smelly. The almost instantaneous connection I feel on meeting them in the woods makes me realize that I am rapidly evolving into a true thru-hiker myself, minus the bushy beard.

It became apparent that the trail was not something that could be done without some definitive push and pull factors. Kirsten was in good company on her recovery mission.

What every true thru-hiker has in common is a reason for being on the Trail—something they are escaping from or looking for. Transfer them into the real world and they would be aimless graduates, lonely divorcees, rebellious executives. But out here on the Trail there is a sense of purpose, companionship, and peacefulness that comes from living in harmony with nature. In the real world they would answer to labels and attachments: Mr. John Smith, MBA, executive director, Gold Card holder, ex-husband; on the trail he is known as Free To Go, his companions Let It Be, White Pine, Californian Coyote.

Before Kirsten left, I had consoled myself with the thought that she would be safer on the trail than on the streets of Johannesburg. I had also airily proclaimed, "Oh, for goodness sake, this is America, there are bound to be outdoor toilets and clean water at every stop"—an example of what my children describe as "Mother's famous last words."

I've figured out how they designed the Appalachian Trail. They drew a line from north to south across the rockiest mountains in the country and threw in a few white blazes to ensure you don't miss out on any of the toughest peaks. Remember that for every inch you trace me along your map, I go up and down several hundred feet.

Tonight we are camping in the woods by a small stream with a northbounder called Totem. Our food bags are strung high in trees, hopefully safe from bears, moose, and raccoons. We are preparing to face the most difficult mile of the entire trail: the legendary Mahoosuc Notch. I look forward to tomorrow with some trepidation; I may have to have two sachets of oatmeal for breakfast.

Later:

I survived Mahoosuc Notch! I scraped my knees crawling up exposed rock faces in strong winds. Then, in full rain suit, hat, and gloves, I climbed the 5000-foot summit of Goose Eye Mountain to be blown right off my feet. Eventually I found myself crawling across the boulders on my hands and knees, with tears stemming from a combination of physical exhaustion and being far from home. Tonight I ache from my feet upwards.

After reading these descriptions I had to adjust my sources of consolation. My first reaction was, "I don't want to know," and yet I did want to know. The pain, emotion, and perseverance were all part of what it took to rebuild a broken body and mind. As the journey continued, I saw evidence in Kirsten's letters of her growing ability to place things in context. Against the background of the vast mountainous landscape she had become a part of, I gained insight to her thoughts and experiences. I compared her adventures with the days when she couldn't remember the names of her own family.

> Met an interesting guy today, Lone Scout. He wanted to know what I was doing so far from home on the trail. I told him I was living. This made me think of the extent to which the trail is a metaphor for life. Plenty of ups and downs, smooth days and rough. I can climb to great heights and be suitably rewarded by the magnificent views and sense of achievement. But often the uppermost peaks are too cold and windy to bear. The downs seem endless, rocky and treacherous. I rely on the encouragement and companionship of other hikers, but remain independent and carry my own load. It is a journey into myself and through myself, toward a self-determined destination.
>
> I write this on a bright cold night as the stars appear through the trees reflected in the shimmering surface of Sabbath Day Pond. Loons call across the water, and an imperfect moon rises above the mountain peaks. I am gradually remembering parts of my past and determining my future.

As snowstorms swept through the Shenandoah National Park and the windchill fell to zero degrees, Kirsten and Bear Charmer were forced off the trail that had been home for five months and thirteen-hundred miles.

Three years later, Kirsten gave up her job as a successful environmental scientist in Cape Town and returned to the trail. She resumed her hike, and Bear Charmer (Sue) joined her, despite having completed her thru-hike in 1996. Unfortunately, a few weeks into the trail, Sue sprained her ankle while crossing a flooded stream. Kirsten continued on her own, with Sue keeping a motherly eye on her and making frequent visits to check on her progress from her home in North Carolina.

> From a poem in the trail register, by Oriah Mountain Dreamer—Indian elder:
> "I want to know what sunshine sustains you from the inside when all else falls away?
> "I want to know if you can be alone with yourself and if you truly like the company you keep within the empty moments?"

I know that Kirsten has got her inner sunshine back. I feel huge admiration for her courage in creating memories to replace those beyond reach, in finding direction to show a way once lost and in trusting in time and nature's ability to heal.

—Kirsten and Lise Day

The Art of Living

My mother-in-law, Jean, died on New Year's Eve. Had it been up to her, I suspect she would have chosen otherwise.

Each First Night for years, she and my father-in-law, George, had celebrated with a circle of friends called the "Bridge Club," which dated back to college days. In recent years, however, Jean had teasingly suggested that she was going to find some new and younger friends. The gatherings were beginning to break up way too early. She loved parties.

When her children were young, she partied with them. She painted cancan dancers on the basement walls in their former house on Pfeifer Avenue and threw birthday parties there amid the boxes and old furniture. At New Year's, she organized a fantastical family hat contest and parade. There were block parties on Independence Day, with brightly decorated bikes and wagons rolling past a reviewing stand full of dignitaries, mainly the oldest people living on the street. She was always the one to plan a party to welcome new neighbors or to say farewell to departing ones.

Jean was trained as an artist. In a box of old papers, I found her college resume. Under "career goals" it said "commercial artist" and "illustrator of children's books." Instead, she accepted a job with the chamber of commerce and married her college sweetheart. She continued to paint, though: still lifes and landscapes of faraway places, cribs and castles and children's furniture, *trompe l'oeil* doorways into secret rooms, murals on nursery walls for her grandchildren. She painted faces at her granddaughters' birthday parties.

Once, she said, rather wistfully, that she'd like to have a show, just once, and sell a few paintings. Just as I always had an idea that I would write children's books and she would illustrate them. It's the kind of thing you never get around to doing, when time stretches away endlessly and there are other claims on the present.

That last sad summer, she'd admitted she was ill right after the annual Fourth of July party and fireworks display. She'd finally allowed her youngest son, her favorite, to take her to the hospital. It wasn't easy. She did not believe in going to doctors, although she had been president of the hospital's women's board. Had volunteered thousands of hours there. Had planned their parties and benefits.

"Don't worry," she had always assured us. "If something is wrong, I'll go."

Later, she said, "I went, and see what happened?"

They kept her for four days before they operated. When they opened her up, they found an inoperable cancer. We took her to a famous hospital for a second opinion, and that doctor was blunt. "If you have anything to do," he said, "do it now."

After that, we were greedy, filling her house every weekend. The kitchen overflowed with food, and their minister became a frequent visitor. George bought her long-stemmed roses, bouquets of white and red and yellow blooms. She even took the chemotherapy, because we'd insisted.

Late in October, she asked us one afternoon if we would take her to Santa Fe, where the artists are. "You and Rod will have to help me. We could sit in the sunny courtyards and go to the Georgia O'Keeffe Museum. I hear there are lots of pretty shops there."

"Yes!" we said. "Let's go now!"

"No," she said, "We'll wait until after Thanksgiving. The chemotherapy will be working by then, and I'll be feeling better."

"No," we begged, "Let's go now!"

She smiled sadly. "I'm too weak," she said.

"We'll push you in a wheelchair," we offered.

She shook her head. I knew she did not want to take a wheelchair to Santa Fe.

That same week, they did a scan. Everything was blocked, her stomach, one kidney.

"It's okay," the doctors said. "We can put a tube in your kidney so it will work again, and we can put a tube in your stomach so you won't get sick, and we can feed you through another tube. That will get you maybe four more months." And the doctors were pleased.

"No," she said, or "No, thank you," perhaps, because she was always polite. "Even though I understand that a lot can be done with tubes these days."

She turned apologetically to George. "We've had forty-nine wonderful years," she said. "We don't need four more miserable months."

And we took her home with an IV for fluids and a fistful of prescriptions. Those were bittersweet days. Jean sat in the needlepoint rocker in her sunny bedroom or on the living room sofa with a throw across her lap, because she was always cold. Her children brought her boxes of old papers and photograph albums. She shared the secrets she wanted to tell and revealed her hiding places. They lifted down her purses full of mad money. She had more than a thousand dollars stashed away. George was baffled. Perhaps it was Santa Fe money.

She was getting tired, sometimes peevish. Her sons did their best to decorate the house for Christmas, but everything had to be rearranged. She became impatient with the IV, and she needed more medication to keep the pain at bay. Her sons and daughter worked shifts, struggling to keep her comfortable.

The Bridge Club rallied around, as did all their other friends, driven by the need to do something at a time when there was little to be done and little time to do it. They felt the sting of a thousand past kindnesses that languished unrepaid. "Can we cook?" they asked, and they did cook. "Can we drive someone to the airport or pick someone up?" "Can we sit with her for a few hours, so you can rest?"

My own parents had both died suddenly and alone. So, I'd always held the theory that if you just kept a close eye on a person, they couldn't slip away on you. It isn't true. We watched Jean grow thin, her flesh melting away as her spirit freed itself. Now when the minister prayed with her, he wept, his tears making dark grey spots on the light grey comforter. Jean worried about him.

"He really shouldn't take these things so much to heart," she said one night after he left. "He'll wear himself out."

She marked the verses in her Bible that she wanted read at her funeral. Her daughter, Nancy, picked the hymns.

A few weeks before Christmas, she issued her orders. She sent Nancy to shop for presents and ordered more from a catalog. She had been resisting sending Christmas cards; now she sketched a design and we rushed it into print. Her sons spent hours addressing the envelopes. They had so many friends.

She no longer fought the IV. She had set a goal for herself. She had always been a great keeper of Christmas, and she would keep it one more time.

The house was full on Christmas Day, as it had been in so many other seasons. She was able to open her presents and to watch us open ours.

The day after Christmas, she said, "I've had enough." And she began to slip away to other places and other times, returning to us less and less often.

Her family surrounded her on the night she died. George and her children were all there, talking in quiet voices, sharing memories when she stopped breathing.

At her funeral, the minister said she had a beautiful life, and she did. She was also fervently impractical. She quietly disapproved of the computer-generated labels on our Christmas cards. She was always gracious, had been raised right. The smallest kindness elicited a card addressed in elegant calligraphy, a personal note inside. It is a way of life we don't make time for today.

After the funeral I stopped to thank one of the church women who had helped with the funeral luncheon. She waved away my thanks impatiently. "I would do anything," she said firmly, "for Jean Chima."

An artist leaves behind a body of work. Jean is no exception. I see her often in my husband, in his love of art and beautiful things, in his ability to create them himself. Like his mother, he cuts beautiful pictures out of magazines and files them for the future. Her imprint is on each and every one of her children. They, too, are works of art, created, in part, by her hands. It is women's work, the legacy of the choices women have always made.

I think it is a story worth telling. There are ways of living and ways of dying, and ways of painting the world as you travel through it. Some artists work in glass and some in fiber, and some work in the lives of those around them.

—*Cinda Williams Chima*

The Courage of
John Bankston

I t was in 1987, during the height of summer camping season in the Texas Hill Country, that John Bankston achieved a more memorable hero status than his considerable sports accomplishments had ever earned him. That year John was just another high school football player at summer camp . . . until the rains came to the Texas Hill Country.

There are more camps in this region than anyplace else in the United States west of the Mississippi River. It is the hill country's version of big business. During the height of the 1987 camp season, July brought an unexpected late season heavy rain and with it the severe flooding that is endemic to the hills.

In Texas it has been common practice to neglect the building of expensive bridges over waterways. People are frequently forced to cross rising floodwaters in creeks and even rivers by using the notorious "low-water crossings." These are laughable but cheap substitutes for real bridges. They are laughable, that is, until the water rises unexpectedly.

In normal low-water conditions, these crossings usually protrude slightly above the surface of the stream. After even slight rains, many of them are under water by a few inches, so vehicles frequently cross at those points through several inches of flowing water.

One such low-water crossing isolates the Pot of Gold Camp from outside traffic, and on one fateful day in July 1987, the rains came. They kept coming, and with considerable force. In the hills, streams can rise perceptibly, even dramatically, in a matter of seconds. It was at just such a time that the driver of a busload of Pot of Gold campers faced the decision to cross or turn back. Yes, the water was rising quickly, but the driver felt he had time to make it. He chose to cross. Big mistake. The light truck crossing ahead of the bus stalled, stranding the bus behind it in the rising water.

The vehicles lost contact with the pavement and the water slowly swept them into the churning, rising turbulence. Panic ensued. Many campers decided it would be best to stay in the bus. Another mistake. The sliding, tilting vehicle quickly began to fill with water, and those who had lingered now faced deeper, faster, and more violent water than had been the case only moments before.

People scrambled for any refuge they could find.

Trees were the most obvious and easiest to reach. But the swelling water carried the frantically struggling campers past several trees before they could manage to catch one and climb to apparent safety. The rain kept falling and the water kept rising. Locals familiar with such floods later estimated that the current reached speeds in excess of sixty miles per hour. Literally within minutes, a tree that seemed like a solid and secure stronghold on which to ride out the tempest became a moving, creaking, bending death trap. Enter our hero.

John Bankston was a high school football star. He was a big boy and very strong. When the water kept rising and the trees that people were clinging to began looking like traps, John started saving lives. One after another, John retrieved them from their precarious, disappearing perches. He laboriously worked his way out to them, loaded them onto his powerful back, and slowly carried them to shore. The current grew increasingly swift and dangerous, filled with sharp and heavy debris, including whole trees that had already been uprooted upstream. But John was young and strong.

The newspapers said he carried several people to safety, but he was unable to get to them all. Some died in the water that day. Many of those he saved would surely have gone with them. One of the campers he managed to save was especially at risk of drowning. The camper was wearing a full-leg cast on a broken leg. It was a plaster cast. The kind you're not supposed to get wet. The kind that gets really heavy when it does get wet. Reports vary, but consistently they mention John carrying that particular camper on his back for thirty full minutes before getting him to safety—a half hour for just that one camper.

There is no telling how long John labored that day in the violently churning water that carried trees past him. In some ways, John was responding like a typical football player. He relied on his strength and his conditioning to keep him going when others might have stopped. He felt invulnerable in his athletic youth, and that same feeling of invulnerability that served him so well on the football field was also his undoing on that fateful day. Somewhere out there in the water, on yet another mercy mission to still another anonymous victim of the flood, John disappeared. Ten died in the water that day. John's body is the only one that was never found.

A pretty good definition of a hero is a person who does what has to be done regardless of the consequences. There are true heroes and there are pretend heroes. John Bankston was the real thing. I never knew John, but I salute him with all my heart.

—Dan Cooper

Counter Actions

Pendle Hill, Wallingford, Pennsylvania, 2001

She asked me to review the story she would read to the class the next day.

"It took me forty years to write it," she said. Her voice was steady, but her hand trembled as she handed me the pages.

Later, in my room, my hands trembled as I read them.

Time stopped as my eyes fell on the topic of her personal essay. My body stiffened as I read down the page. My palms perspired. My head buzzed. My heart raced. My face flushed. Just as they had forty years ago.

During introductions at the writers' conference, we had been drawn to each other as if to magnets that could coax buried treasures to the surface. We sat side by side for the four-day workshop at the wooded Quaker retreat center. With seekers from across the country, we unearthed gems from the soil of our souls.

Although she and I were seeded in the soil of the same region and grew to maturity during the same era, we had traveled different hills and valleys in the South of our heritage. We had breathed different air and had overlooked from different vantage points the vistas of our territory and our time. In the recesses of our hearts, we had clutched, since birth, partial pieces of a map leading to the buried treasure of our people. And with the wisdom granted to children, we each had known that ours could not be the whole picture. Now, in this unlikely time and place, we would retrieve our maps from their protected sites, smooth their crumpled surfaces, and nudge together their jagged edges.

As my eyes fixed on her account of coming of age in the South as a black female, my memory fixed on my own coming of age there as a white female. Suddenly, it was 1961. . . .

As she sat staring down racism at a "for whites only" lunch counter in South Carolina, I sat choking on racism's venom in a high school for whites only in Alabama. She feared for her life. I feared for my soul. She was on the outside, wanting in. I was on the inside, wanting out. Threatening men confronted her in Spartanburg. They brandished wooden clubs and demanded that she abandon her seat. Threatening questions confronted me in Birmingham. They brandished tradition's clubs and implied that I should abandon my stand.

From paths separated by race, tradition, and the state of Georgia, we simultaneously reached jumping-off points. Our respective leaps of faith would lead, forty years later, to her passing half the story from her still hand to mine . . . and to my awakening at 4:30 A.M. to pen the other half:

Woodlawn High School, Birmingham, Alabama, 1961

Would you be willing to have Negro students in your school?
    Very unwilling. Somewhat unwilling. Neutral. Somewhat willing. Very willing.

Would you be willing to speak to a Negro student?
    Very unwilling. Somewhat unwilling. Neutral. Somewhat willing. Very willing.

Would you be willing to walk down the hall with a Negro student?
    Very unwilling. Somewhat unwilling. Neutral. Somewhat willing. Very willing.

Would you be willing to sit near a Negro student in class?

Very unwilling. Somewhat unwilling. Neutral. Somewhat willing. Very willing.

Would you be willing to sit across the table from a Negro student in the lunchroom?
Very unwilling. Somewhat unwilling. Neutral. Somewhat willing. Very willing.

Would you be willing to invite a Negro student into your home?
Very unwilling. Somewhat unwilling. Neutral. Somewhat willing. Very willing.

Time stopped as my eyes fell on the series of questions that lay on every student's desk, awaiting answers before the class could proceed. My body stiffened as I read down the page. My palms perspired. My head buzzed. My heart raced. My face flushed. *Keep your eyes on the questionnaire,* I warned myself. *Do not look up. Do not make eye contact.*

Moment of crisis. Moment of truth.

Interrogators seemed to shout inside my head, as if into a foxhole, insisting I declare my identity:

What is your name? What is your serial number?

An ancient query from my faith challenged me to declare my allegiance:

Who do you say that I am?

Familiar voices swirled around me, rising in jeers and guffaws, falling in mutters and profanity, their waves engulfing me, pounding like a portent.

They gotta be kiddin!
What nigger lover made this up?
I ain't sittin cross from no nigger and watching em eat
. . . makes me sick to think about it!

Familial voices rumbled and then roared storm warnings through my body, pummeling my temples as their volume increased and searing my soul as their urgency intensified. Pastoral voices retorted, ricocheting through the chambers of my heart in a riposte of unworldly wisdom. Served with open heart by forehand from the pulpit and returned with closed mind by backhand from the porch. For years I had whirled across a familiar divide and pounded a familiar surface. Dazed and disoriented, I had spun in a volley of values between pastorate and parentage— batted and battered in a battle between fear and love, tradition and truth, wariness and welcome, curse and blessing. A battle for my soul.

There is neither Jew nor Greek
There is neither slave nor free.
There is neither male nor female, for you are all one.
. . .

> *Carol Jean, our maid is not a "lady."*
> *Jessie is a "woman." We don't say "ma'am" to*
> *women.*

I will pour out my Spirit on all people.
> *No, Carol, the yard man can't eat at the table; you*
> *know Sam takes his plate to the basement.*

Let us do good to all people.
> *Carol, Mrs. Smith said she saw Sam in the front*
> *seat when you drove him home.*

Finally, pushing against the weight of the ages and the aged, a new voice sprouted from the soil of my soul:

What is your name? What is your serial number? . . .
> *Who do you say that I am?*

The engulfing waves suddenly ebbed, as if a riptide were pulling into a distant sea both their pounding and their portent. As the roar of others' voices receded, the new voice, which I now recognized as my own, stilled the internal waves and directed me to plant my feet on the solid soil of the parted sea. Without moving from my seat, I made safe passage to the other shore. Though my hands still trembled from the trip, I marked my answers with certainty:

Very willing.
Very willing.
Very willing.
Very willing.
Very willing.
Very willing.

Forty is a time-honored period of passage: forty years in the desert, forty nights on the ark, forty days in the mountains, forty years on a lunch counter stool and in a high school desk. It seems to take forty to escape bondage, to hang on until the storm subsides, to stare down temptation.

It took forty for two women from different worlds in the same region to "return to our seats" to retrieve stories of an uncivil time: forty for my black friend to summon the courage to sit once again in terror at a counter reserved "for whites only," and forty for me to summon the grace to claim my adolescent declaration as its own counter-act of courage in a whites-only world.

—*Carol Padgett*

What If?

What if, as you made your way home one day, just as you would any other day, from work, or from shopping in your local supermarket, or from taking a stroll in the park, or even, like fourteen-year-old Merima, from school . . . and you turned the corner to enter your street, but where your street used to be, there was a huge, gaping crater . . . and farther up the road, past the dead and wounded bodies, the scarred buildings, rubble, and debris . . . there was the crumbling, smoldering shell of your home . . . and you suddenly realized that everything you once owned was gone . . . and worse, everyone you once loved and shared your home with has vanished, perhaps missing, perhaps injured, perhaps even dead?

It is exactly what did happen to Merima, one of many refugees I assisted during the four years I worked with a small charity in Bosnia and Croatia. Today, a staggering 20 million people like Merima—the majority of them women, children, and the elderly—have fled war, conflict, disaster, ethnic violence, or persecution and are refugees from their homelands. During the time I was working in Bosnia and Croatia, in the early 1990s, the number of displaced people in that region alone was close to 3 million.

Merima was just one of them. Her crime? Simply being an ethnic Muslim in a village coveted by Serbs. I found her—alone, frightened, withdrawn—in an illegal refugee camp at Culineca, on the outskirts of Zagreb in Croatia. The conditions were among the worst I had seen in any camp. More than 6,500 people were living there with no clean water, no electricity, no cooking, no sanitation, and no medical facilities. Typhoid, hepatitis, head lice, scabies, and respiratory and intestinal ailments were rampant, not to mention cancers, kidney and heart diseases, and diabetes.

Merima was shy when we were introduced. She wore a long, tattered floral skirt, a dark red sweater, and a pair of dirty pink bedroom slippers several sizes too big. Her dark eyes were clouded with tears. Unlike most of the refugee children I had met, she refused my hand when I held it out to her. I sat down on the bare concrete floor of her hut and beckoned her to sit beside me. Other children gathered around, curious to find out what was going on. Very slowly, with the aid of an interpreter, I managed to gain Merima's trust and coax her story from her.

"I was naughty that day," she began, dabbing her eyes with her sleeve, "I was wrong, and I shall never be able to tell my mother I'm sorry. I came home from school late—I'd stayed behind to play with my friends—and arrived home about dinner time. It was winter and dark, I couldn't see anything. I didn't know what to do. . . .

"Then someone grabbed me, told me to run with them, told me the trucks were leaving and we had to get on them. There was no time to look for my family. They told me the mosque had received a direct hit; the mosque was right next to my house. They had seen my father come out of the house; they had seen him fall."

Gradually, over two days, I heard the entire story. Prior to the bombing, Merima's two older brothers and father had been rounded up and taken to Tronopolje, one of the worst Serb concentration camps, where they had been subjected to brutal torture. To this day, nothing more has been heard from her brothers. Because her father, who suffered ill health on top of the torture, would likely die in the camp, in a rare show of compassion or perhaps out of embarrassment, his Serb captors released him.

Merima, her mother, and her sister were overjoyed to see him alive. Sadly, their elation was to be short-lived. A week later, the Serbs arrived and started dropping bombs on their village. Eighteen months later, Merima had received no news of her family. She had no idea whether they had survived, whether they were in another camp somewhere, or whether they had all perished together in their house.

I was determined to find out. Merima lent me the only mementos of her family she possessed: a few small, faded photographs kept in her purse. They were not much to go on, but they were all I had. Before I left Croatia I contacted all the main aid agencies such as the UNHCR, the Red Cross, and the Red Crescent. I showed them Merima's photographs and gave them her parents' names; all, without exception, simply shook their heads.

"You'll be lucky if you ever find out what happened to them," Tomislav Muric of the United Nations High Commission for Refugees (UNHCR), told me. "Everything is so chaotic here. Nobody knows where anybody is right now. But good luck anyway."

On my return to England some weeks later, I visited an international Muslim aid group in Birmingham. I heard they had been flying severely injured Bosnian Muslims to the United States and Europe for emergency medical treatment. It was a long shot, I knew. But God or Allah must have been on my side that day. Someone in the charity's office recognized

Merima's family name. He was fairly convinced that Merima's father had been flown on a Medivac flight to the United Kingdom for treatment. I couldn't believe what I was hearing. Could Merima's father actually be right here, in my own country?

I waited for what seemed an eternity as files were scrutinized and names and photographs were compared. Finally, official identification was made, and I found myself ferried by chauffeured car to the General Hospital in High Wycombe. There I found Merima's father, still a very sick man, with her mother and younger sister at his bedside. Then came the problem. How was I to break the news to them that I had found Merima? In the back of the car on the way to the hospital I had rehearsed it time and again, but now that I was actually with her parents I felt tongue-tied.

In the end, unable to find the right words, I simply hugged Merima's mother and pressed photographs I had taken of her lost daughter into her hand. She was speechless. She sat down on the hospital bed beside her husband and wailed, rocking backward and forward, kissing the photographs. Close to tears myself, I made a promise, a very rash and foolish promise, a promise I would instantly regret. Not knowing whether I could possibly achieve it, I told Merima's family I would reunite them; I would return to Culineca camp and bring

Merima back to the United Kingdom with me.

Eight weeks later, I arrived at Culineca. I was horrified by what I saw. The place was literally a bomb site. I was told it had recently been declared a health hazard by the government, a political euphemism for "undesirable," and just the day before I arrived, the entire camp had been razed to the ground by bulldozers. The refugees, I was informed, had been loaded, once again, onto trucks and transported to various other camps around Croatia. Unwilling to board the trucks, some had fled, others had hidden themselves. I panicked: What if Merima was lost? What if I couldn't find her? What would I tell her parents? I couldn't bear to think about it, and shed tears of frustration, disbelief, and bitter disappointment.

Then, suddenly, as if by some miracle, she was standing in front of me. Though a mere child, she was one of the few who had stubbornly refused to leave. I rushed toward her, shouting the good news in English, as though she could understand. She threw her arms around me, sobbing.

I handed her a letter from her parents and an English postcard from her sister. Through an interpreter I explained that, in order to be reunited with them, she would have to travel with me through seven countries and across seven borders, illegally, as I had only her parents' papers and a letter from the Muslim organization to get her through. I told her there could be serious problems and delays, that we might be turned back at any point, and that at the last minute, she could even be refused entry to Britain. But these were risks we had to take.

Merima had never traveled before. She was carsick, frightened, and eerily silent the whole way. She knew little about me, and I realized it must have crossed her mind that she could be the victim of kidnappers. We had no interpreter on the journey to England, so all I could do was hug her, squeeze her hand, and smile reassuringly, despite my lingering fear we would not succeed.

The British border was the one I feared most, and by the time we reached there, I had decided the best thing to do was to smuggle Merima in. I could not risk her being interrogated by some unfriendly immigration officer and turned away because of her lack of papers. Nor could I risk admitting to them that I had already smuggled her across several other borders. So, as we climbed back into our truck after crossing the English Channel, I hid Merima under a pile of sleeping bags. In sign language I told her to keep completely still and silent for at least two hours. I then held my breath as we approached the immigration checkpoint.

Fortune again was on our side. The officers on duty asked a few simple questions but failed to look in the back of the truck and then waved us through.

Hardly daring to breathe, I felt the sweat pouring down the back of my neck. All I could think of was what would happen if we got caught: Merima would be returned immediately to Croatia, and I probably would be arrested. And there would be no family reunion.

But we had made it, the final hurdle. A few miles down the road, when the coast was clear, I called Merima to emerge from her hiding place. "We are going to find your mummy now," I said, hugging her as she clambered over the seat and joined me in the front. I think then that she understood me, for it was the first time I had ever seen her smile.

Finally, two hours later, on the concrete steps in front of their new home, Merima and her family had a tearful reunion.

Among the frenzied hugs and kisses, Merima's first words to her mother were, "I'm sorry."

Merima and I both realized that we had been extraordinarily lucky. Any number of things could have gone disastrously wrong. It helped that I had been sincere and determined and that she had been trusting and brave. Even so, ever since then, neither of us can stop asking ourselves questions, lots of questions, all of them beginning with "What if?"

—Caroline Kennedy

Let's Keep Dancing

The luminous dial on the bedside clock stretches its hands toward three, already two hours past the agreed-upon time. Where on earth is she? For the umpteenth time I peer through the bedroom curtains into the gloom below, hoping for the sight of a taxi rounding the corner, bringing her safely home. Already thoughts of road accidents, muggings, and murder crowd my mind and I torture myself with each horrific scenario until I could literally scream. My nerves are stretched to breaking point. Many more Saturday nights like this, and I'll end up having a heart attack. Not that she would notice, too concerned as she is with her own little world and the latest romance at its center.

In fact, that has been another bone of contention between us lately: men. She just can't pick them. Well, she can, but only the kind who break her heart.

I've lost count of the boxes of tissues she's gone through over some romance or the other gone wrong. The latest, Eddie, is no different, for all I know, but she won't hear a word against him. Although I do have to admit, she smiles much more these days. She thinks I'm overly protective, but just six months ago she rarely left the house. I had to practically drag her around to the shops for new clothes. Now, she's never in, day or night. I suppose I must take some responsibility for the change in her. I was the one who introduced her to the Friday night club at the local community center. Since then, she's become a different person. And I'm finding it difficult to cope with the new her.

Now, I try, really try to be enthusiastic over her sudden interest in fashion. But my interest wanes somewhere between the frilly dresses, especially that awful fuchsia one, the chunky gold jewelry, and the spiky heels. Her friends are equally fluorescent, and to see them all together, sunshades are a must.

She complains that I don't talk enough with her visitors. I would if I could, but I don't understand a word they say. They converse in a language totally outside my realm of experience, using words and phrases that could be the vernacular of another planet, never mind another generation.

I know it isn't easy when they're at this stage in their lives, but I've done my best to bring some order, to give her new interests, and to add a little culture to her world, all to no avail. Dancing is now her number-one hobby. Forget paintings, sculptures, and literature: If it doesn't have a beat, it's not worth a thing.

Suddenly, I hear the sound my ears have been straining for all night. Her laughter floats up through the early morning air as she giggles at some whispered exchange—calls of "goodnight," more laughter, and then the clickety-click of her heels as she totters up the path. Her key has barely turned in the lock before I've crossed the bedroom in two strides, switched on both the landing and hall lights, and am waiting at the entrance. Anger, frustration, love, and an overwhelming need to protect all merge into a kaleidoscope of emotion while I wait to play out what's fast becoming a regular Saturday scenario.

Like a rabbit caught in headlights, she stops inside the door, blinking in the harsh glare. She looks so small and vulnerable. Her tiny, slim fingers appear almost translucent as she raises her hand to shield her eyes from the blinding lights. "Hello," she says.

"What time do you call this?" I reply.

And so begins the usual script. A quick lecture from me, a sigh of exasperation from her, and then off to bed to salvage a few hours of sleep. Only tonight, things aren't running to pattern. There's a glint of defiance in her gaze.

"You won't be waiting up for me after tonight. I'm

moving in with Eddie tomorrow."

My legs feel kind of wobbly, so I sit down on the top stair and scan her face for signs that it's all bluff and bravado. No, she's perfectly serious. She climbs the stairs and sinks down next to me. She sighs gently, and her features soften as she takes my hand.

"I'm sorry I was so blunt. I know this is difficult for you. But I really have to live my own life now," she says in the same quiet, soothing tones I recall from my own childhood.

"Eddie is good for me," she continues. "He makes me laugh, and I haven't been doing a lot of that lately. He may or may not be the right one, but I'm ready to find out. I'm strong enough to look after myself now. You've been so good to me since Dad moved out, but it's time for us both to start living our own lives again."

In the silence I feel her anxiety, waiting for my reaction. Slowly, I realize she's right. For the past year our lives have been on hold as we've struggled to come to terms with the upheaval and tumult that has affected all of our lives but almost destroyed hers. I've spent months urging and coercing her to live again, and now she's telling me I've succeeded. It's my turn to let go, to move on.

A great sense of relief floods through me. I'm no longer solely responsible for her happiness. She's found friends from her own generation who also have an input. That's how it should be. I feel a tremor of excitement at the prospect of making my dreams a reality. I could return to college, take that holiday. . . .

Smiling, I stand, pulling her up with me.

"Okay, Mum, you win," I laugh. "I guess at seventy, you're old enough to go it alone. Now c'mon, let's get some sleep. You've got a big day ahead of you."

"Yes," she laughs. "I'm so happy. I think I'll wear my beautiful fuchsia dress tomorrow. Eddie will be so pleased. It's his favorite."

My mum has, indeed, picked up the threads of her life. She teaches ballroom dancing three days a week at the local leisure center, visits her friends for dinner, takes embroidery lessons, and, of course, still enjoys the company of Eddie. She is a wonderful example of it never being too late to start again, whatever your age.

—*Lorraine Wylie*

Wildfire

With blaring sirens and horns demanding clearance, the fire truck roared around a blind corner of La Tuna Canyon, its noisy haste a familiar but welcome intrusion. Behind us, fifty-foot flames ignited the canyon's chaparral, the wildfire traveling faster than our band of animal rescuers. The long, winding road led to safety but was shrouded in darkness, each step a potential danger for our charges: ten horses fleeing the wildfire, their barn already in flames. We were trying to outrun the fire, but were delayed by a kennel of dogs whose owners had abandoned them behind locked gates. We climbed the fences, lifting each dog out in turn and loading them into the last pickup leaving the area.

Nine of us were experienced rescue volunteers. The tenth, the owner of a bright sorrel yearling, didn't know the pitfalls. She was leading her beloved

Arabian down the middle of the road, assuming it was the safest spot. It wasn't. As the red tanker screamed down on top of her, catching the terrified pair between its headlights, the yearling panicked and darted, dragging her into the darkness beside the road. The woman screamed. We could hear the year-ling thrashing. Then there was only silence. I handed the older gelding I was leading to another woman and ran to help. The sorrel was upside down in a trench washed deep from last winter's rains. He was lying on his back, his legs waving helplessly in the air, his head wedged against a boulder. The fire truck dis-appeared around the next bend.

"Thank God he's small," my daughter Kim said over my shoulder. Quickly, we assigned the other nine horses to five of the handlers and hurried them on their way to safety. The rest of us stayed, trying to figure out how to get the youngster out of his predicament. We gave his owner the task of steadying his head with the lead rope. She'd have to control him once we managed to lift him free.

Kim covered the sorrel's eyes with her jacket and moved aside. When I lifted his head, she moved under his neck, using her legs to hoist both him and her a bit higher. Two of our companions tied ropes to his front fetlocks and pulled hard toward his rear. Slowly, despite his best efforts to rid himself of us, we managed to raise his front end and shift him onto his hind legs. Hoping he was balanced upright again, we hustled away from his flailing hooves. The rest was up to him. His owner pulled hard, trying to get him to scramble toward her. Front legs grabbing at the crumbling bank, he struggled again and again to jump out. The fire roared closer, but still he remained at the bottom of the four-foot embankment. A few more minutes and we'd have to abandon him. None of us hesitated. We rushed back in, shoulders low, pushing into his rump, and collectively lifted him. His hooves found solid ground at last, and he lurched over the lip of the crevice.

"Go, go, go!" we shouted at his startled owner. She bolted, with him running freely beside her. We ran behind, urging him faster and faster, as the fire consumed the area we'd just abandoned and snaked up the opposite hill.

The hills surrounding Los Angeles are attractive neighborhoods for recluses and animal lovers. Away from the bustle of city life, equestrians can spend hours on back trails enjoying the friendship of their horses. Most of the year, the isolated canyons delight residents with quiet trails, the sweet smell of chaparral in bloom, birdsong, and deer sightings. But the attractions of these havens also provide intense danger in fire and flood seasons. The canyons offer only constricted, poorly paved roads—one lane in, one lane out. During a disaster, their narrowness demands all nonemergency vehicles be kept out or shoved aside. I watched one fire truck shove an upturned horse trailer over the edge of a twenty-foot cliff because it was blocking the only access road. Fortunately, the two-horse trailer was empty.

The Los Angeles Fire Department (LAFD) is dedicated to saving homes, humans, and property. They are not equipped and do not have the resources to assume the additional burden of rescuing animals, a task for which they are not trained. Until the 1980s, there were no formal animal rescue teams, only volunteers like us who set up a telephone system to quickly get the calls out when help was needed. Our calls came from Equestrian Trails Corral 12, based in Sylmar, a suburb of the San Fernando Valley in Los Angeles County. We responded in natural disasters around the valley and surrounding areas. Grabbing halters, lead lines, portable cat and dog cages, and anything else that might be of use, we'd pile into trucks pulling trailers and race to rescue the animals in danger, hoping we would arrive in time. Usually, we did, but sometimes we were too late.

The 1981 Brown's Canyon fire raced from one end of the canyon to the other in less than twenty minutes, trapping many horses in their stables. We drove up the canyon amid still-smoldering ruins, hoping to find survivors, fearing what else we'd find. Brown's Canyon Boarding Stable was the largest facility up the narrow road. A popular place, it featured horse shows amid a maze of horse corrals and barns sprawled up and down the hillsides. Close to the road was a large, dirt parking lot that was usually filled with trailers, but not one was in sight. In the center sat a lone pickup truck, its owner sitting with her smoke-blackened head resting against the door frame. The window was open, and she was struggling to breathe. I recognized her immediately. I'd bought my own truck from her a year prior.

"Karen, you okay?" I asked.

She nodded and grinned, gesturing toward the arena. It was filled with horses milling about in confusion. They were wheezing as hard as she, the smoke still burning their lungs, but they were alive and safe from the fire. I handed her a towel.

She wiped the soot from her face and then described having survived a wildfire:

> They stole all the trailers. People from this ranch who didn't own trailers and people from other ranches came here and took trailers that belonged to others. I hooked up my trailer and went to get my horse (she gestured toward the barn highest up the hill) and when I got back, they'd taken my trailer right off my hitch. It was too late to ride him out. The only thing I could think of was to turn him loose in the arena. Then I ran around,

grabbing others and turning them loose in there too. I figured, if they fought with each other, it was better than being stuck in those barns up on the hills. I jumped in my truck, rolled up the windows, and tried to breathe through my blouse. It was so hot, it felt like the air itself was on fire.

Tears wet her cheeks but didn't dampen her smile. Not one horse burned. Karen's quick thinking and courage saved about fifty horses that day.

By the time the Bell Canyon fire roared through, we were better organized. Bell Canyon is a housing tract designed for horse lovers, with a central barn and show area but also with enough acreage at each home for horse keeping. These roads were wide enough and plentiful enough for us to drive into the tract to retrieve the endangered animals.

We decided to drive to the top, figuring the fire would hit there first and we could get the animals from the lower homes later. One woman wanted us to sign a receipt saying we'd pay for her horses in case she didn't get them back. She dropped her request when we loaded up her neighbor's horses instead. A rabbit dashed past, its fur in flames. We knew a new hot spot could erupt nearby at any minute. By then, it was too late to get another trailer up the road, so Kim grabbed the lead ropes of three horses and began running down the road. I followed with four horses in the trailer.

As the fire crested the ridge, Kim realized she couldn't outrace it on foot by following the winding road. Taking a desperate chance, she veered off into virgin land, preferring to run through the brush on a straighter course while I wound my way down the road. We met up again at the bottom, turning all seven horses over to the handlers who'd set up a picket line. We turned the trailer around and made a second and then a third trip with the rest of our team. Every animal we found was saved. Every vehicle and trailer came through in good condition, as did the owners and volunteers.

We weren't so fortunate when the hills close to Palmdale burned. Cathy Decker was our driver that night. Her sturdy truck and metal trailer survived just fine. But the trailer ahead of us sported a fiberglass top. Sparks landed on it as we fled from the fire, igniting the trailer's enamel paint. We watched the fiberglass melt, with two horses inside. The owner of the truck kept going, unaware her speed was fanning the flames. Fortunately, we made it out before the manes of the horses caught fire. As soon as she parked, we slammed open the rear doors and let the horses run backward, out of danger. The entire top half of the trailer was gone within a half hour.

We congregated in front of a roadside cafe, waiting to see if we'd be needed again. Cathy noted that almost all of the volunteers were women, with the few men organizing and the women carrying out most of the rescues. Since the majority of horse owners are women, this is logical. It takes extensive knowledge and experience in horse handling to convince a horse not to panic, to convince it to get into a strange trailer that may smell of smoke, and to lead it along dark passages toward safety.

In the 1980s, Equestrian Trails Inc. (ETI) created a formal rescue squad that received specialized training and cooperative contacts with both the LAFD and the Los Angeles Department of Animal Regulation. Out of our first efforts, an entire system has developed to ensure the safety and survival of animals caught in natural disasters. The local high schools are set up as centers of safety for evacuated animals. Animal Regulation personnel supervise the volunteers who care for the animals until their owners arrive to claim them. Various shelters, both public and private, take the overflow and find new homes for those animals that are not reunited with their owners. ETI, a nonprofit association, still maintains a volunteer database and an organized disaster aid program that continues to save the lives of animals throughout California.

—*Loretta Kemsley*

The Power of Words

The day Scott was born, his thirty-year-old parents felt blessed. They had prayed for and prepared for that special day. Scott's dad, Barry, was a fine arts administrator and high school and church choir director. Scott's mother, Debbie, was a school music teacher and church pianist. Though accomplished in their careers, becoming parents was the ultimate reward. For me, the maternal grandmother, the birth of this first grandchild swelled my heart with gladness.

The precious baby seemed perfectly fine, but he did not progress as expected. Scott could not sit without support or do many other things that infants his age normally do. At seven months, he began having seizures, which caused his development to regress to that of a two-week-old baby. Doctors ran tests, including a CAT scan of his head, but nothing showed up. They described his problem as a chemical imbalance. Later, he was labeled with autism. Like most autistic children, Scott rarely makes eye contact. On the other hand, he loves to be hugged and kissed, which autistic children normally do not.

After having his first seizures, Scott was unable to put weight on his hands or feet. He just lay on his back most of the time. His tenacious mother searched for help. She enrolled him in physical therapy, occupational therapy, speech therapy, water therapy, and music therapy. With the therapists and his parents' constant help, Scott learned to sit alone, crawl, and float on his back in water. His petite mother physically carried her heavy son everywhere.

When Scott turned three, the law required him to attend school. Agony overwhelmed Debbie as she strapped her curly-haired child who could not walk or talk or feed himself into a seat on the yellow school bus. Scott finally started to walk at age five. The walking prayer had been answered, but Scott still could not talk.

Debbie saw a segment on *Prime Time Live* about a mute boy with cerebral palsy who used a computer to communicate. She attended a workshop on facilitating (aiding the person who is typing on the computer by lifting his hand and allowing him to move to the next key). His parents started asking him simple questions, asking him to type *Y* for yes and *N* for no, but he showed only mild interest in the computer. Debbie decided to incorporate Scott's favorite pastime, spinning in a chair, with questions. She showed him pictures on cards, verbally naming what was pictured on each card, later adding words to the cards. She asked Scott which word or picture matched the word she said, and if he pointed to the correct card, she would turn the swivel chair in a spinning motion. After six months, Debbie changed to words-only cards, with no pictures. Holding up two cards in front of her, she would say the word on one of the cards and ask Scott to point to the one on which the word she'd said was written. He got it right every time.

One day Scott was fussy. So, Debbie moved him to the computer and asked, "What's the problem?"

Scott typed. "I am sleepy."

Debbie's tears flowed as she rocked him to sleep.

When Scott was five, his parents and teacher realized he could read. The first book he read was Steinbeck's *The Red Pony*. Every three or four pages, he would be tested for comprehension. Exasperated, he typed, "Quit testing me and let me read."

The second book he read was *Annie Sullivan*. Scott began absorbing everything in his environment. His typing vocabulary became extensive, and he showed evidence of a photographic memory. When his parents asked him how he had learned to read, Scott typed, "By watching TV shows like *Jeopardy* and

Wheel of Fortune." In later years he wrote, "Printed words lay all over my brain." Pretty remarkable for someone who once had been diagnosed as having an IQ of 22 and declared profoundly mentally retarded.

Medical doctors, pediatricians, neurologists, psychologists, psychiatrists, therapists, facilitating aides, and a mind-boggling amount and types of medications have been a huge part of Scott's life. Because Scott is self-abusive, he wears splints on his elbows to keep him from hitting his head. Wearing splints for so many years caused one elbow to become stiff, and so the splits were removed. Since then, he has worn a helmet day and night to protect his head from the hitting. Because he intensely slaps his arms and legs, he wears sweatpants and long-sleeved shirts for protection.

Scott's life has expanded tremendously since Debbie first placed a computer before her seemingly remote and supposedly unreachable son—and released him from an inner prison of frustration, loneliness, and silence. With language, he was able to learn, to make friends, and to express his thoughts, emotions, and dreams. In middle school, he received an award for his writing. That winning essay reads, in part:

Life has been hard for this now thirteen year old. Many therapies have been tried; many disappointments have been felt. But this story is not about tragedy. This story is about triumph. This is Scott's story. This is my story.

I want the same things other thirteen year olds want. I want to be liked. I want good grades. I like nice clothes. I like girls. My school has given me a chance to be normal. Even though I can't talk, I can type. Many people have learned to facilitate with me. I go to regular class and do regular work.

Since most of my life is so weird, I am especially grateful that my school allows me to be myself. Every year my teachers have given me a chance to tell my story to my classes. Instead of laughing at me, the other kids ask me questions and become my friends. As I go through my day, there are students in each class who help me. Some of them might never have paid attention to a kid like me. Some of them might even have made fun of me if they had not been informed.

All of us have special needs. Some are just more obvious than others. What I wish to do most is talk. That is a big dream, but no more of a dream than the short guy who wants to play basketball or the poor kid who would like some nice clothes. Vincent Van Gogh wondered what life would be like if we had no courage. I think we would still be cavemen afraid of fire. With no courage, life is pointless.

Someone a few years ago decided that a kid like me might work out in a regular class. That took courage. Those first teachers and students had to be brave. I hope I have done a good job on my part. It would become a story of tragedy if I was the reason they stopped working with kids like me.

Determined that Scott would have a chance to do what other kids do, Debbie took him to Boy Scouts, church activities, school dances, and Special Olympics, and facilitated him with the drum in the junior high band.

When Scott turned fourteen, the seizures increased, both in number and severity. They were hard. He might have several seizures a day, each lasting thirty minutes or longer, day after day, and every night. At fifteen, Scott had a device implanted in his chest to help control the seizures, but it has had little effect. The seizures continue to control his life.

But the seizures have not curtailed Scott's desire or ability to communicate, as you can see by this excerpt of Scott's writing when he was fourteen:

My most memorable experience is learning to facilitate. My world changed after that. I plotted to talk, but it was not to be. When I first started typing, my parents were crying. I was excited because now they could understand me. The neighbors and adult friends came to facilitate me. I tried so hard. I was interviewed for a newspaper story. One coach didn't believe I could type. He thought the person holding my wrist was doing the typing. He made me mad, but then I tried even harder because I knew there were always going to be people to convince. That first facilitating experience is still special. The future looked brighter, and I had escaped my cell.

At age fifteen, Scott wrote this about his aides.

My relationship with my aides is important to me because I am dependent on them. They help me with my work and my daily living. I am physically strong and worrisome, so they have to be strong, too. I try to be good and help them, but sometimes I know I don't. Pass out the patience. They have to have a lot of it. I know how lucky I am to have them.

I'm glad I've had people behind me who push. Sometimes my physical self and my mental self don't agree. My mental self says, "Sit down and be quiet," but my physical self says, "Run out the door." If people only looked at the physical me, they would give up pretty fast.

I had some therapists when I was little who were very demanding. They set the goal. Since then, my teachers, my friends, and my parents all look to my mental person. I wish the mental side could be in charge all the time, but it is not to be.

What would have happened to me if people had not been determined and pushed? I might not walk or facilitate. Thank God for people with determination.

This May, Scott turned sixteen. A month later, he completed his sophomore year of high school, right on time and with academic honors. In an award-winning essay he wrote for his English class, he concluded:

> *Words are wonderful. I know I am lucky. So many kids like me live locked-up lives. What I wish for them is finding the key to their locks like I did.*
>
> *My greatest dream is to talk. But I thank God for the gift of language . . . no matter what form it takes. Let my courage show.*

We see your courage, Scott. We hear your words. In sharing them here, may others gain strength from them, too.

—*Emmarie Lehnick*

Keys Made of Ivory

We often think of heroes as persons who risk their lives to save others. But sometimes our heroes are the role models who have helped shape our lives by their examples. Let me tell you about one such hero, my mother.

As she slept on the fire escape to catch any limp wind that might make a stifling hot New York City summer night less uncomfortable, she noticed the stars. Inside the open window five stories up, in a building with no elevator, was a bedroom shared by five children who all attended PS-28. Their mother slept on a day bed in the parlor.

As a girl, my mother recited "Evangeline" to the darkness, hummed tunes, and imagined what it would feel like to stroke the silky fibers of a puff-sleeved dress that had not been handed down from a relative's closet. She also figured out how many coins she'd need to buy a doughnut filled with strawberry jelly. To her, the metal of the fire escape felt not like iron bars but like a gilded birdcage, and she was the songbird.

"Twinkle, twinkle, little star . . . " Her hazel eyes would look upward, past the tenements' tops to the Milky Way, searching for silver flickers in the night.

For five cents, she could see a chapter from the "Perils of Pauline" at a movie theater on a Saturday afternoon, if she could find an adult to purchase the ticket. This treat was worth the chore of waiting in line for coal for the stove used to cook and, in winter, to heat the apartment. A movie was a luxury, but music a necessity.

The street sounds of women singing in Yiddish, Italian, French, and so forth provided a merging chorus of cultures. Each lullaby was also a remembrance of a home or loved one left in another country. Though Caruso was idolized in the opera world, the women rocking their babies, repeating the soothing sounds of the generations, gave her more satisfaction. She, too, would continue the legacy of homeland songs, passing them along as gifts to her own children.

Music. Wealthy women traveled in elegant horse-drawn carriages and used powder puffs made, for income, by poor widows. But even the poor could listen to the magic of instruments and voices blended into a beautiful composition.

In a middy blouse and navy skirt, she learned to play ivory keys that spun notes and chords like precious gold as felt-tipped hammers struck strings of stretched metal. With dexterity, slender fingers depressed keys, weaving rich tapestries of music.

"I can earn money, Mama, by teaching piano. I can earn enough so we can have a collection of twenty-five-cent pieces to run the apartment gas meter."

Did her mama stroke wisps of hair and smile at a twelve-year-old's American dreams? Did she see in her young daughter, as in Evangeline, that: "*Something there was in her life incomplete, imperfect, unfinished; / As if a morning of June, with all its music and sunshine, / Suddenly paused in the sky. . . .*"*

How many pennies did it take to buy frail white ribbons to place in a thirteen-year-old girl's shiny hair, primping for her debut performance at Carnegie Hall? Was she nervous? Was she filled with disbelief? Had she wished upon a star for such a situation, where the powdered women in fine attire would settle in luxurious seats to listen to her?

My mother was thirteen when she stepped onto the stage at Carnegie Hall and played the piano, "*Sweeter than song of bird, or hue or odor of blossom.*"* With a dancer's grace, she slid from the wooden bench to accept the audience's applause. A sliver of satin ribbon touched her cheek as she nodded to the crowd. No one before had ever worn that ribbon; no one in her family had ever performed at a world-famous music theater. No one in the audience knew about her feather bed shared by five siblings, about the fifth-floor walk-up tenement, about hand-sewing the dress she had performed in. And no one cared . . . about anything except the talented teen who had provided such tender music.

As I now sing the same lullabies to my grandchildren that my grandmother sang to my mother, I feel privileged to add another link to the song of generations. But my mother taught me that the darkest, most stifling night need not be filled with grime and despair; there are always stars if one looks through the clouds. My mother encouraged the endless possibilities of imagination and made me understand that dreams do come true sometimes.

My father died suddenly at age forty-five, and my mother elected to remain alone and celibate for the remaining thirty-two years of her life. With grace and a smile, she found employment and raised and educated her daughters. Without complaint and without burdening loved ones, she died a painful death from contaminated blood received after open-heart surgery. To the end, she reminded me to listen to life's music.

Whenever I have moments of self-doubt, I've only to go into my living room, sit down on the wooden bench upholstered with her handmade petit-point cover, and play melodies from my childhood on the baby grand my father bought her in 1939. Four generations have made music on that instrument, which we've always called, and still do, "my mother's piano." Her legacy. We've each our own "Carnegie Hall" dreams, and as I slipped a sliver of pale satin into one of my granddaughter's blond strands, I knew my mother's philosophy would continue. And as I sit in my air-conditioned kitchen, I enjoy doughnuts filled with strawberry jelly and tell my grandchildren stories about a strong, sensitive, spunky woman who searched for twinkling stars and created magic on keys of ivory.

—*Lois Greene Stone*

"Keys of Ivory" was first published in the spring 1994 issue of *Mature Years*.
*"Evangeline," Henry Wadsworth Longfellow

A Year in the Life of a Heroine

I learned a lot about courage this past year. I didn't learn it from soldiers, although there were many fine examples from which to learn. I didn't learn it from firefighters or police officers, although among them are certainly exceptional heroes. No, I learned courage from Kay—and it was a lesson I'll never forget.

In May 2002, Kay's doctor suspected she might have breast cancer. The long, warm summer passed in a whirlwind of tests combined with her job as nanny to twin toddler boys. Her hour-long commute to and from work was often filled with fear, tears, and prayers. Yet those who know and love her saw a different side.

She told me about the possibility of the cancer only after the biopsy had been taken. "I'm probably just fine," she reassured me. "I'll find out in a few days."

Upon returning from a Labor Day weekend get-away with my family, I learned the news. "I have breast cancer," she told me, in a calm and clear voice.

I didn't know what to say. This couldn't be happening to Kay. Well into her fifties, this petite blonde was filled with spunk. She had energy and enthusiasm that far surpassed my own and that of most people I know. Her optimism was contagious, and her love of life—especially with regard to her family and friends—was fierce. She couldn't have breast cancer. It simply wouldn't be fair. After all, she looked and sounded just fine. She said she even felt fine. But she wasn't. And true to her character, she had waited to tell me until after our return from vacation.

"I didn't want you to worry," she said in her no-nonsense style. "There wasn't anything you could do by knowing my diagnosis before your trip."

As usual, she was right. It didn't make knowing any easier. I couldn't imagine what knowing was like for Kay, her husband, and her three grown children. I couldn't imagine what I'd be like if I were in her shoes.

Kay, however, strapped her shoes on with dogged determination. She stood up proud, squared her shoulders, and started taking the steps needed to fight the disease. First, she armed herself with one of the best weapons every fighter needs—knowledge. She researched, read, asked questions, and studied—not only her disease, but available treatments, their side effects, and their statistics with regard to remission.

Armed with an already strong faith in God, she now wore it like an armor of courage. Then, she simply started filling her arsenal. Once she, along with her husband and her doctors, agreed on a course of treatment, she had surgery to remove the cancer. Just two days after surgery, she welcomed her son and his fiancée home for a weekend visit. A few days after that, she returned to work—caring for and instilling her good values in her rambunctious twin charges. In fact, she worked throughout her radiation treatments. Arranging to have treatments in a hospital near her work, she simply altered her daytime routine with the boys.

"I have it all worked out," she told me before returning to work. "I can't lift the boys to put them in their cribs, but they can climb. So, I'll put chairs by their cribs and they can climb in. Then I'll move the chairs so they can't crawl out."

She was, of course, a savvy, experienced mom.

"Then I'll rest when the boys nap," she said.

She learned to let the piles of laundry she normally folded and immediately put away remain unfolded in the laundry room. She learned to shut off the phone ringer and, as best she could, to turn down her mind. She knew that rest was necessary for her healing, and she was determined to heal. She was blessed with a boss who empathized with her situation, joined in arming her for battle, and was grateful she could still care for the twins.

Optimism sat side by side with Kay's faith and knowledge—ready to defeat any foe set loose in her path. While enduring her treatments, she eagerly anticipated and planned for her son's marriage in the spring. When her spirits lagged, she bolstered them with ideas for a mother's gown, shower arrangements, and excitement about her son's plans. She encouraged her youngest daughter to apply to college, and she remained her middle child's closest confidante. She maintained close ties with her dear friends. I wonder whether she had any notion she was teaching courage to those of us observing her? I doubt it.

When treatments ended and tests confirmed that Kay—not cancer—was the victor, her family and friends shared in the relief and joy that comes with facing down danger at close range. When prayers, shared and powerful, are answered, the presence of God is apparent. But the presence of God was always apparent in Kay. Her goodness and honesty were catching and offered openly to anyone willing to accept her gifts.

On May 10, 2003, Kay's son, Christopher, and his bride, Joanne, were married in a beautiful, spiritual church wedding. The joy of the young couple's union was shared by all in attendance, and there was not a dry eye in the church. The greatest joy for me—and I know for many of Kay's relatives and friends, especially her dear husband—came when the mother of the groom walked down the aisle. Accompanied by a handsome usher and trailed by her faithful husband, Kay fought for composure as she walked down the aisle and lit the unity candle on the altar. Some wedding guests saw a woman wrought with emotion. After all, her first child was being married. Some saw a nervous mother and soon-to-be mother-in-law, as she struggled to contain her tears and trembling.

But I saw courage. I saw a year of what could have been lemons turned to lemonade. I saw a strong woman become even stronger. I saw determination in the face of danger and a will to overcome that danger like none I'd ever witnessed.

Yes, I learned courage from Kay. And I pray if I ever need to put it into action, I'll fight as gracefully and with as much strength as she did.

—*Kimberly Ripley*

The Ultimate
Power Pole

Like a condemned woman, I stood at the base of the power pole wondering why on earth I had put myself into this situation. At this stage, I had only one real choice: upward.

At the introductory evening, the course organizers had assured me I could cope. I was not so certain. I got vertigo just standing on a stool, my terror of high places ran pretty deep, and my fitness level was definitely suspect. Just team building, they'd said, a course to bring out your leadership skills, a nice group of people, trained instructors, and, of course, no compulsion to do anything you don't want to do. Fear of heights? Not a problem. We are here to help you.

The setting was superb, I had to admit that: gleaming white sand, sea and sky aglow with the turquoise and pinkish silver of sunset, and an unpretentious wooden building in the sand dunes. My single room was simple and clean. Through the open window I could hear waves swishing on the beach. But I like my personal space, and the noisy animation of arriving students outside my door, plus the thought of three days of regimentation and determined togetherness, were beginning to feel like boarding school. I sat on the edge of the bed, feeling strange and out of place, wishing I still smoked.

That first evening, we had all introduced ourselves. There were twenty-four of us, men and women, mostly in their thirties, all confident, outgoing, fit-looking—except for me. I was forty-eight, overweight, short (just five feet, three inches), unathletic, and full of self-doubt. The next day's activities began with breakfast at 6:30 A.M., uncomfortably early in my book.

Much to my surprise, I enjoyed day one. We played energetic team games on the beach, kayaked, and found the fastest way through obstacle courses. In the evening we mellowed around a beach bonfire. I fell asleep feeling secure, pleasantly warm and fuzzy, ready for more.

They say fear is all in the mind: Tell yourself you are not afraid, and you won't be. Well, it's not true.

Day two was cliff climbing and rappelling. I worked hard at prebreakfast tai chi, trying to generate enough life force to get me through the day. All I generated was tears. I cried as I froze to the face of the cliff like a swatted fly. I cried as I clung by my toes to the top of the cliff, heels hanging into space, with no possibility whatsoever of climbing back up the rope. I cried with sheer relief when I reached the ground. My fear of heights in top gear, I was in shock. Too emotionally exhausted to appreciate my achievements of the day, I missed dinner. I just wanted to be alone. I was still asleep when the breakfast bell rang the next morning.

On day three we trailed across the sparse, prickly grass after the instructor.

"Today, folks, we're going to climb a tree. It will be fun; you'll all feel like kids again."

Yeah, well, I was a kid and I never, ever climbed a seventy-foot-high Norfolk Island pine, nor have I ever, including now, wanted to.

"There are twelve of you, so we'll have someone strong go first and last. The rest of you rope up in between."

Desperation was making me cunning, and I quickly stationed myself between Neil and Pete, two guys who seemed capable of making it up and back down the tree. Like a gangly, uncoordinated caterpillar on a foraging expedition, the team ascended and returned earthward.

I forged an intimate relationship with that tree. With my heart beating wildly, I embraced it passionately, gripping it to me with feverish fingers, my body pressing into its every curve. Neil and Pete allowed me to use their limbs as branches to compensate for my lack of reach. I felt inadequate and frustrated, failing completely to appreciate the subtleties of working as a team.

After dinner and multiple glasses of wine, Neil and Pete felt safe to tease me, and in due course, it did all seem quite hilarious. The organizers were right: This was a great bunch of people. But as for the promise of not doing anything I didn't want to . . . hadn't they noticed?

Tomorrow, day four, was the last—Armageddon.

The instructors stood in a group, serious, like observers at an execution. Four power poles, barely noticed until then, quickly became the highest, most intimidating power poles I'd ever seen. A trapeze with fluttering yellow ribbons had been attached between two of the poles, and from the others hung businesslike festoons of ropes and metal hooks.

"This is a personal challenge; you don't have to do it, but I suggest you all try. The idea is to climb to the top, stand up, count to three while the rope holders get ready, leap forward, and try to grab the trapeze. The ropes will hold you, but you need to jump away from the pole."

Three people gave definite refusals; I wavered. The show-offs had already climbed up twice, blindfolded. I willed myself forward and into the harness.

If I didn't do this, two days of misery would have been for nothing. I shut my eyes and reached for the first handhold. It was my forty-ninth birthday; it could be my last.

I heard the instructor's voice gently urging, "That's right, just keep going, don't stop. Reach up with your right hand, up a little, a bit more, there. Don't stop, you're doing well. C'mon, you can do it. Only four to go and you're there. Keep your eyes shut if that helps. Don't stop. That's it, that's the last one, you're at the top. Now, get onto your feet. Yes, you can do it. No, you won't fall. Your right foot, that's it. Now the left one. Now, straighten up . . . stand up."

What am I doing? I'm crouched on top of a power pole, a pole hardly wide enough for my feet. I'm going to be here forever; I can't stand up. I can't. If I stand up there will be nothing to hold on to. Oh God, why did I do this?

Shuttered behind closed eyes, I felt strangely disconnected from the panic trying to break in. A clear, quiet voice said, "Pretend you are sweeping the floor. You bend down with the dustpan and brush, pick up the sweepings, now just stand up and throw them in the rubbish."

And I did. I just stood up.

"Now, open your eyes."

And I did. I looked out away down the beach, out to sea, away into forever. I felt weightless. I felt free. I felt unafraid. I felt fantastic.

"Count three and jump for the trapeze."

Arms stretched out, I soared off the pole like Jonathan Livingston Seagull practicing his dive. The ropes jerked me back to reality, catching my fall, and lowered me gently to the ground.

Dazed, high on endorphins, and surrounded by a chorus of congratulations, I asked, "Who told me to pretend I was sweeping the floor?"

They all looked blank.

"Did someone tell me to open my eyes?"

They looked at each other and shook their heads. I don't know where the calm, clear voice came from. All I know is, that day I won a clear victory over fear. And the woman who drove home the next morning was a twelve-foot-tall Amazon.

—*Gillian Wakelin*

 Love's Imprint

"I have to get help," my mother said. "No!" I gasped. "Don't leave me."

"Hang on till I get back. You'll be all right."

She didn't know if that was true, but she knew she had to go.

At nineteen, I thought I was indestructible. Working with horses, though, meant danger always shadowed the next gallop, the next jump.

On a typical hot and humid July day on Long Island, Mom and I did the sensible thing—we went to the beach. She straddled Captain, a trusty quarter horse borrowed from the stable, and I sat astride my own Sasha, a flighty thoroughbred mare.

I was fit and rode every day, so was very confident in my abilities. Mom was a good rider, but didn't get enough hours in the saddle to be truly secure, so keeping a close watch on her was important.

At the private beach, a secluded and deserted strip of sand bracketed by salt marshes, cool water beckoned. I guided Sasha into the calm expanse of bay until she was chest deep, while up on the beach Mom watched from Captain's back.

Sasha balked, as she always did. She didn't like the water, or perhaps it was the uncertain footing. But as usual, she went on at my insistence, her whole body tensing with each step. I'll never know what spooked her that day, but suddenly, she leapt for shore, panicked, and went down, thrashing.

My first thought was simply to get out of her way. I slid off, but with Sasha's legs churning like pistons, I couldn't find my footing. Then, she heaved up her front end, and I got sucked beneath her belly with a whoosh, and she jumped out over me, using my chest as a spring board. I watched her right hind hoof rush straight at my face and felt it ram my sternum and force me under. The momentum of the blow propelled me to my feet, and I lurched toward dry ground.

I started to say, "I don't want to die," but couldn't complete the sentence, because I could not draw a breath.

My mother flung herself from Captain and hit the ground running, reaching me as I collapsed. Sasha made a beeline for home, some four miles through woods and across a busy road. Mom swore as Captain easily broke the flimsy branch his rein was hastily tied to and followed.

Her nurse's training served us well. She checked my vitals. Pulse weak but regular, no bleeding, and I had started to breathe. Each painful inhalation, however, made it clear that things inside were not right.

"Something's broken," I said. The sun's glare in my eyes forced them closed.

"Stay awake. Concentrate. Let's get you in the shade."

"Hurts to move my head. Can't lift my arms."

My mother got me to my knees. Careful to support my neck, she dragged me under the sparse protection of a bush at the edge of the dunes and gently laid me down.

"I have to get help."

Anguish etched Mom's features when I begged her to stay. But I was grievously injured and though she wanted to be by my side, she forced herself to go. The trip required hiking through deep sand in high riding boots on a 90-plus degree day with humidity to match. All she knew was she had to get help, even if it killed her.

And I worried it might. I imagined her dropping dead on the way. I also pictured Sasha and Captain splattered by a truck on the busy road they had to cross on their headlong race for home. These morbid thoughts entertained me while long, graceful strands of beach grass, blown by a welcome breeze, tickled my face and horseflies feasted on my exposed skin.

Later, I heard how Sasha galloped into the barnyard, eyes wide with the excitement of a full-out run, sides heaving, sweat slathering her neck and sides. That was unusual enough—my horse never returned without me—but in the fray, one stirrup had come off the saddle, and spotting that, a stable worker, Jaime, knew something was wrong. Jaime jumped on another horse and came after us.

Telltale hoofprints led the way at the turnoff trail for the beach. Jaime's suspicion was quickly rewarded when she met Captain, his reins broken and dragging on the ground. She grabbed the bridle and tugged him along, thinking something had happened on the road. The next sight shocked her. My exhausted mother's tear- and sweat-streaked face spoke volumes.

"Candace . . .," she panted. "At the beach . . . Get help. . . . Now."

Jaime released Captain and spun her mount around, kicking his sides for speed. Mom was left trying to get on a fidgety horse with only one rein, in her sock feet. Unable to run in the boots, she had ditched them along the trail. Alone on the beach, I struggled to stay conscious, concentrating on each carefully shallow breath and the even rhythm of broken bone scraping broken bone in my chest.

Jaime and a few others jumped in a car and reached me before the ambulance. They found me under the bush, partially buried. To fend off the biting insects, I'd repeatedly tossed handfuls of sand in my face. My mother met us later at the emergency room, where we learned my sternum was fractured in two places. It could have been much worse. The water had cushioned me. And to think that just a week before, I had been riding in the same water at the same beach—alone.

I was thankful for many things that day: to be alive, to not have permanent damage, for Sasha—though she'd nearly killed me, her fast flight home had brought help quickly—for Jaime's fast thinking. But it was my mother's act that demonstrated the complex interlacing of courage and love. That combination provided her fortitude to overcome a powerful desire to stay with me and stamina when she thought she could not take another step. It sustained her for days as she watched a respirator do my lungs' work until I could breathe safely on my own.

Thanks to my mother, I have more than just a faded hoof-shaped scar on my chest to remind me I am not indestructible. Deep beneath that mark, the imprint of my mother's courageous love is permanently stamped on my heart.

—Candace Carrabus

Encounter in Yucatan

Buying a hat would have to wait. More urgent matters were on my mind as I tried to rid myself of the feeling that I was being followed on that Yucatan street. The flight from San Francisco had been delayed for several hours in Mexico City, and I was short on sleep and exhausted from the long trip. I had that spacey feeling that makes you question your senses, so when I began to suspect that someone was shadowing me, I told myself it was just my imagination. Now I decided it could be true after all.

The bright Mexican sun had felt good as I waited for the local bus outside the small airport terminal. Now, as I walked to my hotel carrying my large purse and a small duffle bag, it felt oppressive. My lightweight cotton dress stuck to my back, and the dampness under my arms was prickly. I shaded my eyes with my hand and promised myself that later I would buy one of the hand-woven hats I saw for sale in some of the shops along the way. But first I had to do something about this guy following me.

Don't be ridiculous. Be sensible, my logical self said to the part that was scared. *Why would anyone want to follow you? You're carrying an old canvas bag, not an expensive suitcase, and you're not wearing clothes or jewelry worth stealing.* I realized, however, that I stood out from the other people on the street. For one thing, I was paler than anyone else. Living in the California fog belt, I never developed much of a tan, and everyone around me was much browner than I was. They were all shorter, too. I had to duck my head for most of the shop awnings that overhung the sidewalk, and the heads of most of the men I passed on the street came about to my ear. It was clear that I was a tourist and that I was alone.

But I was certainly not a rich tourist. I had saved for a year to make this trip to southern Mexico. I had been interested in the Mexican pyramids ever since I took an archaeology class in college. The chance to visit them and to go someplace warm in December was very appealing, even if it meant traveling on a tight budget. I had taken a city bus rather than a cab from the airport into town because it was cheaper, and then had to walk several blocks from the bus stop to the modest hotel where I had reserved a room.

No one on the street would have known that,

though, as they saw me striding down the street, anxious to get to a cool place where I could take a shower and get some sleep. What they saw was a middle-aged woman, obviously a stranger and alone, carrying a small travel bag over one shoulder and a purse over the other, with enough funds to journey a long way from home and probably plenty more money on hand. My follower had apparently made this observation and assumed I wouldn't notice him behind me.

I had noticed him, though, in my peripheral vision. He had been walking several paces behind me, always keeping the same distance between us, for at least two blocks. I made some assumptions of my own about him: that he wanted something from me and that he would try to rob me or ingratiate himself with me, maybe try to pick me up. But I needed to confirm that what I thought was happening really was. Was someone actually following me, or was I putting together innocent circumstances that would make a good story when I got home?

How could I find out? I cursed myself for not having been more disciplined in studying Spanish. Without the language, I couldn't confront the guy verbally. I would have to check him out and get him to stop following me without the benefit of language.

Get a hold of yourself, I thought as I walked along, my heart beating erratically and my hands sweaty, not from the heat. *Okay, first I'll slow down to see if he walks past me. If he does, I'll stop worrying.*

I slowed. He didn't pass. I was still scared, but I felt a tiny bit less afraid, realizing I had some control of the situation. I took a deep breath, pulled my shoulders back, and shifted the weight of my suitcase to make it more comfortable.

With my newfound courage, I began to toy with my follower by altering my pace, walking fast for a while, then slowly, and stopping occasionally to look in shop windows. This bought me some time to consider how I could end the unwanted relationship. After a couple of more blocks I crossed the street. He crossed the street behind me. By now any doubt I had about what was happening was gone, but I was still curious about his motivation. I also wanted to see what he looked like.

Crossing the street again, I noticed a store with windows that provided a wide-angled reflection of the scene behind me. I stood in the exact place I needed, peered into the windows, and, yes! There he was. My heart still pounded, but I felt more empowered now that I could see him, and I pretended to study the window display for what seemed an eternity, getting a good look at him. He seemed even shorter than the other locals, had a wiry build, and was perhaps in his mid-twenties. The idea that he might be trying to pick up a woman who was a head taller and probably twenty years older was laughable, and I realized the importance of losing him before he tried to rob me. But how?

By that time we had walked several blocks together, with me leading and him following, and had reached what seemed to be a major shopping area with fair-sized clothing and department stores. These stores opened directly onto the sidewalk, without any glass or doors. At night they were closed by pulling down the grating that made up one entire outside wall. During the days, when the grating was up, people who might otherwise have stopped on the sidewalk to chat stepped into the shade and relative coolness of the store. I saw that I might be able to use this setup to my advantage and began to think of a plan.

My heart still beat rapidly as I looked at the groups of people standing in clusters of twos and threes along our path, but my step was firm and I speeded up my walking pace. I wanted some people to see my plan in action—both to embarrass my follower and, hopefully, to give me support if I needed it.

When I saw a cluster of three men in the shade of the store's interior, I thought, *Now! Here's my chance,* and quickly stepped just past them. My pursuer cooperated beautifully, as, intent on not losing me, he followed on my heels. When he was directly abreast of the men I had just passed, I suddenly stopped and whirled on him. He nearly ran into me, and I was now literally right in his face, in front of a group of his peers. His terrified eyes raced from side to side as he sought an escape route, but there was none.

"Get lost!" I said in as loud a voice as I could muster, towering over him and poking my index finger toward his sternum so emphatically I nearly poked a hole in it.

He got the message, even though I wasn't speaking his language. He opened his eyes wide and raised his brows in that universal expression of innocence and said something that I translated as, "Who, me?"

"You," I said, stabbing my finger toward his chest again. I turned on my heel and strode briskly away.

I walked for a block, eyes straight ahead, before I turned and looked back to see whether he was still there. He wasn't. I stopped and put my bags down. At last I could heave a sigh of relief and wipe my wringing wet palms on my skirt. I stood on the hot sidewalk, forcing myself to relax, until my heart resumed its normal rhythm and my breathing slowed down. Then, I shouldered my bags and resumed my search for the hotel. Tomorrow I would buy a hat.

—Ruby Long

I Thought I Could Fly

As I opened the front door, my mouth dropped open as I saw my three-year-old jump from the top of the full-length stairway. Legs and arms flying, head over heels tumbling over each step, she finally landed at the bottom, and what had seemed like a slow-motion movie scene switched back to normal speed. I knelt by her side, expecting pain and screaming, but to my surprise, she simply rose up and shook herself.

Ami was normally a level-headed child, even at three, and a stunt like that was peculiar for her.

"Why did you jump from way up there?" I asked.

Resting on her elbows, she answered in a perplexed tone, "I fought I could fly!"

Little did I realize that would become the theme of her life.

Most parents claim that it is only by the grace of God that their children become productive adults. It is from that same perspective that I just happened to say something that ended up affecting my child's life.

When Ami was young, we would occasionally have formal dinners with the china and crystal and proper manners. Being a tomboy, Ami would grump, "Why do we have to do this?"

Inside I fumed, "Doesn't this child realize all the trouble I've gone to for her training? I just want her to know how to act in public. Kids need to learn some manners."

During one such exchange, my irritation grew with each thought. When Ami again complained, "Why do we have to do this?" my words came out without thinking: "Because the Bible says, 'When you go before kings and governors' . . . God will give you what to say, but I want you to know how to act!"

I had no futuristic picture in my mind; I was just using the biblical reference to get her to take my efforts seriously. After she became an adult, she shared with me how those words helped to shape her life goals.

"Mom, when you would say that I was going before kings and governors, something deep inside said, 'I'd better get ready, I will be with international leaders.' Those words always stayed with me."

Even though Ami squirmed and complained through the "manners dinners," she began to expect early on that her life had a purpose. She had a glimpse of her destiny—she would go before world leaders.

Her first week of high school she made a list of goals for the four years ahead of her. The list included straight A's, editor of the school paper, speech team, math team, and drum major of the band. I was amazed, and thought if she achieved some of them, I would be pleased. We've always encouraged our children to do their best, but we never pushed them to make the top grades. When she graduated, each item on the list had been checked off.

The World Youth Congress was held during her junior year. Ami was thrilled when she received notification that she was a delegate. That week changed her life. Up to that point, all her efforts had been centered on music, but as she listened to the heart-wrenching stories of teenagers from around the world, her life took on new direction. Suffering had never been real to her until that week. The reality of the world situation took on faces and personalities.

During her junior year of college, Ami was accepted for an internship in a refugee camp oversees. I had a hard time agreeing to her request to go. We were a typical Midwestern family; where did she get her adventurous spirit? But her persistence won out.

Once there, she refused to live in the dormitories. Instead, she moved in with a refugee family with two young daughters. The mother had died and the father had fled his country seeking political asylum. Ami learned the lifestyle and cooking of their culture and eventually learned of the corruption in the leadership of the refugee camp. She learned that the girls of the family had been raped. One day the camp commander called her into his office and said, "If you value your life, you'll keep quiet." Her host family later made it to the United States, and both girls graduated as valedictorians of their classes.

I have often wondered what she would do with a major in political science. Her first job was with World Relief. It was no surprise to find her tiny apartment full of refugees newly relocating to the Chicago area. Strange smells would come from the kitchen as they cooked exotic foods. Beds on her floor were no problem; they were just happy to be in America. She and her husband, Paul, took them in until they secured housing and jobs.

In 2001, she was appointed to President Bush's task force for an African nation. Now, her travels are often to dangerous areas. On one trip she flew a cargo plane into the African bush, sitting behind the pilot on bags of grain. When the pilot signaled turbulence, she had to hold on to the pilot's seat to stay in place; there are no seat belts on a bag of grain. Her duties included inspecting the clinic. The medical facility was the only source of treatment for miles. It was housed under an open structure of thatched roof and bamboo framework with chicken-wire walls. A chicken strutted across Ami's path as she entered. An eye operation was underway, and she was invited to watch. Eye disease was rampant due to lack of hygiene.

It was supposed to be an in-and-out visit into the village of several hundred people; the plane was to return later in the day to fly the relief workers back to their hotel for the night. But such volatile areas are unpredictable, and due to bombing in the area, she and her party had to spend the night.

The villagers used the occasion for a special ceremony, killing a goat in honor of the American visitors, dressing in full ceremonial attire and dancing around a huge fire. In the midst of a food shortage, these people offered their best to the visitors. Late that night when the fire burned low, Ami was shown to her *touk,* a grass hut with a dirt floor. As she entered the door of the hut, a foxhole caught her eye, a reminder that these gentle people's lives were not all celebration.

After all the excitement of the day, the straw mat was a welcome sight. Bugs of unknown species buzzed around her mosquito netting, and the night air was stifling. Just as she drifted into a deep sleep, shouts brought her back to reality. Instinctively, she jumped up, ran outside, and flattened her body into the foxhole. For a long time she lay there in the dark, smelling the muskiness of the dirt, listening to the bombs in the distance, wondering if they would explode over her. Thoughts of her husband and family back home flooded her mind. Prayers went up. They must have been heard, for this was to be a good night. No bombs hit close to the village. (Later, after Ami's departure, bombs did strike the village, leaving many homeless.)

Early the next morning she awoke to the chatter of men's voices in a dialect that was vaguely familiar. She was able to translate enough sounds to know that something big was up and it involved her. When she stepped out into the sunlight, some men of the village eagerly displayed a six-foot python they had just killed right outside her hut, and they were still hunting. Pythons always travel in pairs.

Another African tribe honors her as the "mother" of their tribe at their yearly tribal council. The whole tribe had been slated by their government to be killed; through Ami's efforts, they were able to get out of their country just before the executioners arrived. Eventually, they all made it to the United States.

Through the years I've received many phone calls from Ami telling me about her meetings or lunches with different ambassadors, senators, and various national leaders from around the world. She then reminds me of my words to her so long ago:

"When you go before kings and governors . . ." I always respond, "Well, did you know how to act?" She chuckles, remembering my efforts. And I smile, remembering that when you think you can fly, the sky's the limit.

—*Linda Henson*

Westward, How?

Standing on Chicago's Union Station platform, I took a deep breath and boarded the Empire Builder to begin the journey of my dreams. I hoisted my suitcase up into the overhead compartment and then sank into my assigned seat, placing my pillow and small bag next to me. Somewhere on another car, everything else I owned in the world was packed in two trunks. I felt a small jerk as the train began its trek across the Midwestern states to the West Coast. Shivering with excitement, I settled cozily into the space that was solely mine for the next two-and-a-half days.

Thirteen years earlier, my family had come to the United States from the Netherlands right after World War II and settled in Grand Rapids, Michigan. The next year, when I was ten, I wrote to the Chamber of Commerce of every capital city in my new homeland and asked them for information about their state. I received back a generous assortment of brochures, postcards, and books with photographs, all free.

After weeks poring over information, my dream of settling in Oregon began. In my mind I fashioned a village by the ocean. Our house, complete with picket fence, which I would share with my husband and two sets of twins, had a view of the beach and was shaded by firs and cedars. Behind the house loomed tall, snow-peaked mountains. Our lives would be impossibly happy.

I packed away those dreams, exchanging them for the reality of school, jobs, and getting a teaching degree. By the time I had finished a semester of my senior year at the University of Michigan, I had barely thought of where I would teach. Grand Rapids? I was sure I could get a job there.

In the fifties, school districts all over the country sent recruiters to talk to graduating education majors. I made appointments with representatives from Midwest cities relatively close to my home: Chicago, Detroit, Milwaukee, all logical choices. But then on the list I noticed Long Beach, California, and I thought, *why not? It's the West. Was that vivid, naive dream of my childhood possible?* I had a long conversation with a woman from Long Beach, and she as much as hired me. "My dear, I'm not authorized to make a final decision, but if you want to start packing your bags . . . " But I wasn't ready to make up my mind, and I soon realized that my heart was still set on the Pacific Northwest, if not Oregon, then perhaps Washington.

Although no recruiter had come from Portland, Seattle, or any other Northwest city, I decided that was where I really wanted to be. After researching salaries in that region, I narrowed my choices to three cities in Washington and wrote to the districts in Olympia, Bremerton, and Bellingham, stating that I wanted to teach junior high school.

Each sent back application forms, but Bremerton requested a letter, as well. They wanted me to answer three questions: Why did I want to teach? Why, of all age groups, was I choosing junior high? And why did I want to come to the Northwest?

Women entering colleges and universities in the fifties had two or three fields open to them. Teaching was one of them; another was nursing. I explained that I was not a fan of exposed blood, mine or anybody else's, so nursing was out of the question. I wrote that my experience as a student teacher at a junior high had shown me that junior high kids had dropped out of the human race and I felt it was my mission to help them find their way back. They seemed to like me and gave me an acceptable, if marginal, amount of respect.

It was what I wrote about mountains, I later learned, that earned me a modicum of fame in the Bremerton school district. I explained that I had never seen a mountain in my life. That the highest point in The Netherlands was a few hundred feet above sea level, and that Michigan had a bump in its topography, all of five hundred feet high, that residents dared to call a mountain. I understood that real mountains were often covered with snow and that they probably looked different from white clouds on the horizon. I surmised that mountains were three-dimensional and wanted to know what it felt like to be surrounded by them.

The letter traveled around the district, and just before spring break, I received a phone call in my dorm, from Mr. Jarstad, the Bremerton superintendent of schools.

He asked if I could come for an interview. I told him that this was, unfortunately, impossible, because I had no money.

"I like your voice," he told me. "If you want the job, it's yours."

"You mean I'm hired? Just like that?" I asked.

"You are. Just like that. We need someone at Coontz Junior High to teach English and social studies. Will that suit you?"

"Of course!" I said, hoping my enthusiastic squeak masked my terror.

Of course? I truly have no money, I thought, as I hung up the phone. My parents had no idea that I had even applied for a position so far from home.

My stomach, which had never been happy with sudden emotional upheavals, lurched. I bolted for the bathroom, just in time.

I went home a few days later. "I have a teaching job for next year," I announced during dinner, in a sort of ho-hum fashion.

My father looked up from his plate and smiled. "Congratulations! Where? Grand Rapids?"

I stared at him and at my mother. "Not Grand Rapids."

Mother put her hand over her mouth, and then said, "Oregon!"

"Bremerton, Washington."

"Where is that?" they chimed in unison. On another planet. Somewhere between Jupiter and Saturn.

Mother voiced her dismay. Even cried a bit. That was her job. But this was an irreversible situation, and she knew it. From then on, I had their support.

They could not help me financially, so that summer I worked several jobs and scraped together enough money for a train ticket, ferry ride, hotel for two nights in Seattle, one month's rent, and enough for food and other essentials to tide me over until I received my first paycheck in October.

Then, there I was on a brilliant day in early September, on my way to fulfill my dream. The Empire Builder sped west across Wisconsin. I climbed to the observation deck and gazed at the grandeur of the Mississippi and ate a sandwich Mother had packed for me. By that time, I had become acquainted with others in my car. Robert, an Englishman traveling to Seattle and then down the West Coast, kept shaking his head, saying, "It's so big! So vast! Unbelievable."

From time to time I entertained two small boys while their mother escaped to the bathroom or napped in her compartment. I dredged up songs and games from my babysitting days, and the three of us had a gleeful, noisy time. Our fellow travelers who scowled at us were, no doubt, Midwesterners, taking short, fearful tours of the Wild West. Those who smiled were, naturally, Westerners going home. My soul folk. Future neighbors.

Toward nightfall, I stretched out as best I could across two seats and settled in, thankful for the pillow my mother had insisted I take along.

The next day we traveled across North Dakota, where miles of wheat fields continued, hour after hour. After a while, tired of the "endless waves of grain," I pulled a book out of my purse—Ayn Rand's *Atlas Shrugged*. A week before, I'd found it, washed up on a Lake Michigan beach, waterlogged and with half the cover torn off. Also missing was a chunk of pages, including the first part of Chapter One. Starting on page thirteen, I muddled through the next fifty pages until I got the gist of the story. I tried to sympathize with Dagney Taggard, traveling across the United States on her father's Reardon Railroad, brooding about the shallowness of society.

We entered Montana, and the terrain became slightly more diversified. I closed the book and, shoving Dagney and her angst deep into my purse, I stared out of the window with renewed anticipation.

Some time in the early afternoon I saw my first mountains. Tiny dark shapes appeared on the horizon, so slight, hardly anything more than a defining line, but different from the blue sky meeting flat land, which I had been seeing for more than a day.

An hour later, I could discern more than mere silhouettes. The hills had contours, valleys, shadows. Evening approached. Still, I stayed upstairs, drinking in every detail, until we entered the pass. No moon shone on the elusive landscape, and soon, I could see nothing but my reflection in the dark window.

I went back to my seat, grateful that the space next to me was still unoccupied, and created a nest for the night. My pillow cushioned my head against the side of the train while I pretzeled my legs across the extra seat.

The rhythm of the wheels over the rail seams, now so much part of my life, lulled me into sleepiness, and I realized my fantasy was becoming real. I could no longer see anything, but I knew I was in the midst of the Rockies.

When dawn turned to daylight the next morning, the train was well on the western side of Washington's Stevens Pass. Cedars and firs blanketed the steep hills of the Cascades on either side of the train, and I felt not only encircled by my fantasized mountains but wrapped into their folds. Nothing I had ever experienced in my life came close to that sensation.

I knew one person in Seattle, and when I arrived at the King Street Station, Mia and her friend Al were there to greet me. After storing my trunks, we toured the city.

Mia worked in the Norton Building, at that time one of the tallest in Seattle. We rode the elevator to the top floor and climbed steep stairs to the roof.

All day, I had watched Mount Rainier with amazement, as it seemed to move from one part of the skyline to another. Between buildings. Peeking over a hill. Popping up at the end of a street. Crisscrossed by telephone wires. Now my view was unobstructed. The day was glorious, the sky a dazzling blue, not a cloud. Only my tears blurred the overwhelming vision of this god of mountains.

Beyond Rainier, I saw the snowy peaks of Adams and St. Helens. To the west, the rugged skyline of the Olympics was etched in pink. Mia pointed to Mount

Baker in the north. To the east rose the Cascades I had crossed by train. I was surrounded by mountains, my impossible dream realized.

Looking down at Elliott Bay, I saw a green and white ferry churning through the sparkling water. Tomorrow, it would carry me across Puget Sound to my new life.

I was home.

—Annemarieke Tazelaar

Angel of Courage

At Christmas last year I received from my son and his wife a lovely figurine, an Angel of Courage. They said, "You are the most courageous woman we know."

They didn't know me when I was a five-year-old girl too frightened to go on stage when picked as "the cutest child" at the county fair. They wouldn't have thought me brave when I refused to go to college because I didn't know the ropes and was too intimidated to admit it. They wouldn't have thought of me as courageous when I was the one girl in my high school class who'd found it easier to succeed at nothing than to try and then fail at something.

What they recognize as my courage came later. And it came from my hero, my one love, my husband, and the father of my children—Vern C. Downs.

Yet, I don't think he thought of himself as a man of courage, either. In his mind, a hero was a strapping gentleman, six feet tall, and handsome as a movie star. Five feet, seven inches is more like it, with broad muscular shoulders, carrot red hair, and freckles. He had bowed legs and walked with a slight limp. He drove a Ford truck. And when he was a kid, his nickname was Tuffy. I happen to know it took courage to earn that title, but he didn't call it courage; he called it survival in a world that wasn't always fair.

Both of his parents were dead by the time he was six. His mother died from complications during the birth of her eighth child. His father was careless with grasshopper poison he'd used to anesthetize his gums and jaw after having a tooth extracted. When his parents died, Vern and his four brothers went to live at his uncle's farm, a quarter of a mile from our place. Their three sisters were scattered to relatives in three states. One of those girls he would never see again.

By the time he was fourteen, he'd lost his second set of parents when his dear aunt and uncle passed on. He didn't talk about it much. He just said, "Thank God for Uncle Dwight and Aunt Maude."

The first time I saw him, he wore a green plaid shirt and bib overalls and stubbornly refused to stand up to sing with the other kids in the country school we attended. He later told me, "Miss Amoth said if you're going to sing, stand up. I wasn't going to sing, so why should I stand up?" He had that simple philosophy about everything.

A sense of fairness accompanied this boy of courage. I remember a basketball game we attended. A bigger, taller kid wanted to sit where I was sitting, which caused a little ruckus. My hero calmly escorted the troublemaker outside. My red-haired friend was the only one who returned to the gym. When he laughed, crinkles appeared at the corners of his blue eyes. When anger seethed within, the blue eyes clouded gray, and it was best to be elsewhere.

The ship he served on in World War II was sunk off the coast of Okinawa on May 4, 1945. He survived by walking off the sinking ship into the oily waters of the Pacific Ocean. One hundred-fifty of his shipmates died that day. Vern suffered a blast concussion when the ship exploded in the water, but he was one of the 185 survivors. He was nineteen years old. He said, "I was lucky."

He was a compassionate twenty-six when we married. The first goofy thing I did after the wedding was fall asleep while driving his car. We landed in a snowy ditch in South Dakota on our way to the rest of our lives. I cried with embarrassment. He just smiled and said, "Maybe I should drive."

He suffered still another severe loss when our baby girl was stillborn. Though heartbroken, he told me gently, "We'll have more." We had four sons. He had an eighth-grade education. He was so proud when all four boys attended college. "I hope they won't have to work as hard as I do," he said.

He labored with road construction companies, and over the years he worked his way up from laying pipe for a dollar and a quarter an hour to being a trusted and respected head mechanic. I thought money was to spend. He had the courage to save it. His goal in life was to lay the foundation for my welfare. "If something should ever happen to me, I don't want you to scrub floors just so you can eat."

I was devastated when he was diagnosed with myasthenia gravis, a condition in which messages fail to transport between nerves. He had trouble chewing and swallowing. He took it in stride and said, "We play the cards we're dealt." Two years later, at the age of sixty-four, he learned he had stomach cancer. When the doctors opened his abdomen to remove his stomach, they found the cancer had spread and did not complete the surgery. Not once did he say, "Why me?" Instead he said, "I've had forty-five years that my buddies on the U.S.S. *Luce* didn't have."

I believe each life has a defining moment that determines how the rest of that life is lived. His occurred when he was six years old. God took his parents, but substituted a package of courage, compassion, and dignity. My moment came when the end of his life was imminent. I stood by his bedside as he struggled to raise his hand to his forehead in a farewell salute to me and, with a smile in his eyes, raised his lips to kiss me good-bye.

He lived his life with optimism and a courage born of sorrow. That salute was the passing of a torch to me. I carry it proudly. Since I lost my captain, I find myself stretching my abilities. I now am aware that trying and failing is better than failing to try. I now dare to go out of my comfort zone to attain a goal.

This past semester, at the age of seventy-five, I attended a college class filled with people the age of my grandchildren. Life challenges me on a daily basis. I dare to write stories from the heart. I stand with knees shaking before crowds to share those stories. I feel his presence with me always. Those are the times when I think about the losses he dealt with in his life and the measures he took to live through and rise above them. Through his eyes and his example, I learned to find the good in all things, no matter how hard the situation.

If that makes me an Angel of Courage in my children's eyes, I accept the compliment with joy and thanksgiving. I had a great teacher.

—*Betty Downs*

Live

The old clock Kurt had brought from Austria struck 5:00, reminding Magda that he would soon be home. Tonight their family and Reina's would light the traditional Christmas candles on the noble fir and sing "*Stille Nacht*." The peaceful, festive scene reflected in the window—the tree decorated with traditional wax candles, wooden figures, and red crepe paper favors; the coffee table laden with bowls of chocolates and bright oranges—triggered in Magda a painful memory of a Russian December in 1944. . . .

As she forced her icicle-stiff fingers from the pick handle, Magda flattened her lips to stifle a cry of pain. She flexed her coal-dusted hands, blood forming paths over frostbitten knuckles, and shoved them into her tattered coat. Her fingers tingled as feeble body warmth restored circulation.

"*Uhh*," she groaned, as a heavy boot plunged her crouched figure face-first into a loosened pile of coal.

"Lazy Slav!" The guard snarled.

Magda straightened slowly and clutched the pick, barely resisting a suicidal urge to smash it into the leering face. She pulled out a rag and dabbed at her nose, still tender from another similar incident, and licked a salty trickle of blood seeping into the corner of her mouth. When the buxom guard moved on, Magda turned toward Reina, ten yards down the tunnel, and signaled *V* for victory.

Her sister raised her shovel and silently mouthed "Live." Magda muttered their sign for the stubborn will needed to survive until the impending allied victory. Surely then, the Russians would be forced to release the Slavic prisoners whom Hitler had granted Stalin for ignoring his invasion of Poland.

Wasting muscles strained with each black lump Magda dislodged. Her numbed brain nursed a worry: *If Kurt survived the war, would he want to marry a skeletal girl with an ugly twice-broken nose?* And the other fear: her periods had ceased long ago; Reina suspected the vitamin tablets served each morning with their bread and thin gruel. The white pills were rumored to bring premature menopause, thus ensuring slave labor uninterrupted by menstrual flow or pregnancy.

Some of the women sold themselves to Russian soldiers stationed at a rest and recuperation camp nearby. Such degradation gained them soap, chocolates, cigarettes, clothing, and warm gloves. Magda and Reina rejected this method of easing their physical discomfort, though whoring grew more tempting with each passing month.

Reina prodded the prisoners to practice good hygiene and to keep spirits from sinking, to sing or count as they worked. "*Ems, zwei,*" Magda mumbled with each thrust, using the German of her parentage rather than the Romanian of her native country.

She ground her teeth, worn from curbing rebellion, a pressure release prisoners could not afford. Terror of separation from Reina kept Magda's pick moving. She couldn't survive losing her sister again. Last year, Reina had been sent to another mine after she'd harangued the commandant for medicine for a dying prisoner.

Reina was allowed to return only when it seemed certain her sister would die of influenza. The commandant had guessed Magda's condition accurately. She had decided death would be no worse than bare existence.

She remembered Reina shouting, "Eat!" while forcing watery soup dotted with chunks of vegetable skins into her mouth. "I promised Mother we would come home together. *Live!*"

A whistle shrilled, and Magda dropped her pick. Moving like a wooden figure on her village's town clock, she bent to retrieve it, starting when a familiar hand on her shoulder made the world suddenly lighter.

"One more, little sister," Reina said softly.

"Yes. We survived another day." Magda hugged Reina as they walked toward the checkpoint. "How long . . ."

Reina whispered, looking straight ahead, so as not to attract the attention of the scowling guard at the mine's entrance, "Our suffering will soon end. It is near. There are rumors."

"I see no indication of that."

"There," Reina pointed toward a knot of uniformed men, "Russian soldiers, healthy ones."

"When are Russians reason for hope?"

"I overheard two guards say that Hitler's armies are retreating." Reina glanced about to see whether anyone could hear. "The Americans draw near the German border."

Magda gingerly touched her nose. "As we're treated worse than the commandant's horses!" She spat on the path and ground the spittle with her foot.

"The guards said," Reina leaned closer, "that they must increase production this month, because the allies will insist upon our release."

"A month? What is the date?" Magda pictured the rude calendar they had drawn on the fabric lining of their valise. "December sixteenth? . . . We won't be home for Christmas."

The girls parted at the edge of the compound. "Get our towel while I beg soap from one of the whores," Reina said. "Hurry or the hot water will be gone."

Magda walked toward the barracks, thinking about the luxury of her weekly shower. Near a cluster of men at the corner of her building, she stopped and sniffed. *Could a broken nose play such tricks as this? Oranges? Someone had oranges. One of the soldiers? Who else would have such rare fruit?*

Memories of Christmas filled her thoughts. Her mother's polished silver bowls mounded with oranges and chocolates, the fragrance of freshly baked *kuchen*, the tree twinkling with lighted candles. Her senses played mad tricks. She had to find the oranges; the quest to satisfy this obsession overrode fear. Long ago, she had stopped fearing death. Now, she struggled through each day for Reina only.

A thin man wearing a dirty uniform with several crudely mended tears leaned against the building. She edged closer. Not him . . . just sour breath. There, by the water trough, the Cossack holding an officer's horse. His coat pockets looked lumpy. She moved closer, her nostrils flared, sniffing. The scent of oranges overpowered odors of the horse and the soldier's long unbathed body.

"Do you have oranges?" She asked in halting Russian. "I have not seen them in three years. Might I just touch and smell one?"

He scanned her figure, shrugging. "I could use you, little Slav. I wager your nose could ferret out a rabbit for my supper!" Glancing toward his comrades near the fence, he nudged her to the other side of the horse. "Here. You look more starved than I." He slid two small oranges into her pocket, and then shouted. "Go, slut! I have no urge to sleep with bones."

The soldiers muttered obscenities as Magda scurried around the building with the oranges buried in her coat pocket. When she reached her bunk, she tore a small slit in the rotting mattress and pushed the fruit into the straw.

"Where have you been?" Reina shouted from the doorway. "We'll shiver in cold water. Must you take so long to bring our towel?"

"Dysentery kept me in the latrine," she lied.

Each day after that, Magda's punished body endured additional torture. The commandant expected greater quotas and extended the work day by two hours. To bolster failing energy from the laborers, he increased their bread allotments. Exhausted, the sisters had to force themselves to eat anything at all before stumbling into their bunk. Reina bartered what they couldn't swallow.

Magda touched the precious fruit every night,

relieved it had not been stolen. While the small oranges were fresh symbols of hope and strength to Magda, Reina grew more gaunt and silent daily. Magda wandered, *Should I share the oranges with her before Christmas?*

No news came through the underground, and the Russian soldiers moved to the front. On December twenty-fourth, Magda awoke more stiff and cold than usual. She cuddled against Reina and tickled a thin rib, bringing a familiar groan.

"The commandant said we may leave the mine two hours early for Christmas Eve." Magda shivered out the words as she pulled on remnants of woolen stockings.

"I hope vodka flows freely to the guards today and doesn't make them surlier," Reina said as she shuffled out the door.

Reina's wish for plentiful vodka was granted. The two guards nearest the sisters were so sleepy when the whistle blew that they were barely able to stamp the laborer's passes.

On the way to the barracks, Reina stooped to wrench out a small pine seedling, which she tucked into her coat. A smile creased the black dust on her face. "Our Yule tree, little sister. I pray the Allies escape their Belgian entrapment."

"What trap? What have you heard?"

"When the guards were drinking to the health of

the Russian armies, they discussed a German offensive in Belgium and . . ." She smiled, her eyes bright and secretive.

"You know something else, Reina. Tell me!"

"I keep that for your Christmas gift. Hurry. We have a small thing to celebrate tonight."

After eating the scant evening meal of bread and cabbage soup laced with a trace of sausage in honor of Christmas, the sisters went to their corner of the barracks. The other prisoners had deserted it for promised entertainment in the dining hall. They permitted no religious services, but the commandant and guards joined the carol singing during holidays.

Magda pulled a monogrammed linen handkerchief from the lining of the suitcase, tears forming at this reminder of their father, an early war casualty. Thieves had missed it when stealing the sisters' blankets, spare underwear, and blouses. Now, Magda spread it over the scuffed leather valise.

Reina slipped the tiny tree from under her coat. It wobbled in her drinking cup filled with dampened soil. Grinning broadly, she fished a small candle and a wooden match from her side of the mattress.

"This, I got for yesterday's extra bread."

Magda laughed for the first time in months. "Don't light it yet. And turn your back." She took the two slightly shriveled oranges from their cold hiding place and placed one on each side of the handkerchief.

"Oranges! Magda, you didn't—" Reina sputtered.

"Because a Cossack had little taste for skeletons, my chastity is intact. He gave me the oranges out of pity. Joyous Yule, dear Reina." She kissed her sister. "Now let's relish our first fruit in three years."

Reina lit the half-burned candle. Holding hands, they bowed and muttered a prayer for the blessing of being together. As reverently, they peeled the oranges and savored each section.

Magda broke the silence. "Shall we save the skins for another day's treat?"

Reina squeezed the peels, nodding.

"Now, my gift," Reina said, eyes shining, as she thrust a scrap of paper into Magda's hand. Through clamped lips she explained, "This came today from . . . our source."

"Kurt's handwriting!" Magda quickly read the few short sentences saying he loved her and giving instructions for finding him in Austria. She glanced about the room and stashed the scrap of paper in the mattress.

Reina snatched it away and burned it in the candle flame. "We dare not jeopardize Elena's life. Freedom may be months away." She blew out the candle and secreted it in her pocket.

Magda smiled, feeling alive for the first time in years. "I hear singing."

When they were freed six months later, Magda and Reina fled to their village, only to find that their mother had died and members of the new communist government were housed in their family home. The sisters sadly placed flowers on their parents' graves. Lacking proper papers, they slipped away, scarcely breathing as they illegally crossed borders.

Magda found Kurt waiting at a rendezvous in Austria, still anxious to marry her despite her altered appearance. Reina sought and received displaced person status and passage to the United States. Two years later, she found sponsors for Magda, Kurt, and their little daughter.

The clock chimes jarred Magda to the present. Lifting the twisted red paper to her nose, she sniffed the faint odor of oranges from two tiny shriveled skins nestled inside. She placed it on the tree and stooped to adjust a bow on a grandchild's package.

So many gifts, she thought, *they couldn't know the luxury of eating one small orange.*

Nor, God willing, would they ever know, firsthand, the bravery of two young sisters who shared the gifts of oranges . . . and hope.

—*Mary Brockway*

Steady as She Rises

The plane left Boston's Logan Airport right on schedule, lifting off over the deep blue waters of the Atlantic before banking and heading west into pure radiance. It was a picture-perfect day for flying—unless you had a terrible, secret phobia.

"Mommy," my ten-year-old niece Jo whispered. "The man next to me is crying deep inside, like a puppy."

Her mother, Mary, tried not to stare at the well-dressed man in the aisle seat. Leaning down until her ear was right next to her daughter's lips, she whispered, "What do you mean, Jo?"

Usually when Mary flew to Indiana to visit her parents, her own little family occupied the seats six across. She had been filled with trepidation at the thought of leaving her husband, Chuck, in charge of Tim, eight, Max, seven, and Will, five. At the same time, she wanted this outing to be special for Jo, who had just recovered from a long bout of pneumonia that had hospitalized her for four excruciatingly frightening nights.

It had worried her when Jo had passed on the window seat, saying that she'd probably sleep the whole way anyway and her Mom would get to see the landscape for once. Now, with the thought of a weird, whimpering man sitting inches away from her exhausted daughter, Mary felt her heartbeat accelerate uncomfortably.

Yet, the stranger looked perfectly sane, conservatively and neatly dressed in a navy suit, white shirt, and navy tie with fine red and white diagonal stripes, his sandy hair a little gray at the temples. His eyes were closed, as if he had decided the most practical thing to do was to catch up on his sleep during the flight, even though he had a wafer-thin computer case balanced on his lap.

"I don't hear anything, sweetheart," Mary whispered into Jo's ear, afraid that her little girl might still be sicker than anybody had realized. What if Jo were hallucinating, imagining strange sounds coming from the dignified businessman beside her?

"Mommy, look." Jo jerked her head a little toward the man.

Mary looked and felt a surge of relief mixed with pity for the stranger. His hands were clutching the armrests with fingers so white she thought the knuckles could pop through the taut skin at any moment. She relaxed. "Let's just let him sleep."

Jo nodded a little and shut her own eyes. Mary watched her for a moment and then rested her own weary head against the seat. She fought off the temptation to call home, where Chuck's mother would be bustling around the house preparing dinner, or to call her husband at his office. Instead, she dozed off, but when the plane hit a pocket of turbulence, her eyes flew open and she heard herself gasp, "Chuck!"

"It's okay, Mom," Joanna said. "It's just air."

Mary felt the reverberation of metal all the way up her spine, jiggling her senses and shattering her sense of peace. "I know." She sat back, resisting the temptation to grab Jo's small hand. "You relax, honey. It's nothing."

Another bounce sent all the passengers scrambling for their seat belts even before the captain's calm voice reassured them that everything was fine.

"Buckle up, honey," Mary said to Jo, trying to keep her voice from trembling.

But Jo was leaning over the man in the aisle seat, asking, "Mister? Mister, are you okay?"

Even Mary heard the groan escaping from the poor man's pale lips. "Jo, let the flight attendants handle this," she said, watching his eyelids flutter. "Just let him be, honey."

"Mom, he's scared," Jo whispered in the same tone of voice she used to reprimand Max for teasing Will. Then, in the tone she used to comfort her baby brother, Jo said softly, "It's just a little air wave. It's over now, see?"

The man's eyes opened warily as Jo's warm, little hand patted his. "What do you know about airplanes, young lady?" he managed to ask.

Although Mary immediately took offense, her daughter just laughed. "Not too much," she admitted.

The white lips curved upward a little. "You're an honest kid, anyway."

"My name's Jo." Before Mary could stop her, her daughter said, "And this is my mom. You can call her Mrs. Clark."

Both the man and Mary laughed. "I'm Mary," my sister-in-law said reluctantly. "And don't feel you have to talk."

The man frowned a little and introduced himself merely as Dale, adding, "I never talk on flights. Too busy praying."

"I know what you mean," Mary said. "We don't talk to strangers, anyway, do we, Jo?" she added for good measure and turned her face toward the window to prove it.

"He's not a stranger," Jo piped up. "At least, not now." She swiveled in her seat a little. "So, Dale, want to know why I'm not afraid to fly?"

Mary heard him grunt. "He's not feeling well, Jo," she warned. "Why don't you read your book?"

"What are you reading?" Dale asked.

Picking up on the genuine interest in his voice, Jo started to tell him all about old Hepzibah's penny shop in the ancient house with its seven gables. "I love Nathaniel Hawthorne," she confided. "He lived just a few miles down the coast from where we live. We go to Salem all the time."

The color was coming back into Dale's face, Mary noticed. Almost absentmindedly he released his grip on the armrests. "That's pretty advanced reading for you. What are you, nine, ten?"

When Jo emphasized that she was ten, Dale shook his head a little. "That's great," he said almost to himself.

"So, anyway," my niece said with the determination that had brought her through such a frightening illness, "the reason I'm not afraid to fly is because I know how to sail."

Dale laughed. "I suppose that's kind of a riddle, right, Jo?"

Jo shook her head. "No, it's the same principle," she expounded, not a bit self-conscious. "That's why early airplanes were called airships. It's because the air is just like water and can hold up objects the same way the ocean holds up a boat." She leaned toward

Dale a little more. "I don't get scared every time my dad's sailboat bobs a little, so why would I be afraid when the plane does the same thing?"

Dale was flipping open his laptop, and Mary thought Jo had worn out his patience. "Jo, honey, why don't you read a little?" she repeated.

"I'm going to write that down," Dale said. He looked at Jo, and I can imagine what he was thinking, since I've had the experience myself of looking at Jo's shiny brown hair and marveling at the busy brain beneath. "Better yet, why don't you?"

Jo put down her tray, and Dale deposited the laptop on it. "What should I write?" Jo asked.

"Just what you told me," Dale said, and watched as Jo's fingers tapped out the letters. "And you know how to use a computer, too. Amazing."

"Don't you have kids?" Jo asked.

Mary sat up straight, afraid Jo had gone too far.

"They're older," Dale explained. "Twice your age and then some."

As Mary relaxed again, the plane jittered a little. While Dale let out his breath, he didn't grab the armrest. Instead, he watched my niece write down her explanation of the physics of flight.

When she stopped, he asked, "What do you know about lightning? Or fireflies? Or blenders?"

Jo stopped writing only when the plane landed smoothly on the tarmac, surprising all three of them.

"It's been the best flight I've ever had," Dale said. "Jo, do you think your mom would give me your address and phone number?"

Mary let Jo give him both, and then they both shook hands with him.

"I hope you never get scared in a plane again," Jo said solemnly.

"I don't know about that," Dale was honest enough to say, "but I do know one thing for sure. Whenever I do, I'll think of one brave little girl."

Mary and Jo forgot all about Dale during their visit and only remembered him on their flight home, but he wasn't on the plane. Once they were back in the little town of Rockport, Jo went back to school and Mary resumed her duties as a full-time mom.

About a month after their trip to Indiana, Mary got an excited phone call from the director of the town's public library. She had received a letter and a current catalogue from a senior editor at one of the country's largest publishers of children's books, telling her that she could select $1,000 worth of books as a donation to the children's room in Jo's name. Of course, the editor was Dale.

The local newspaper did a story about the gift, and Jo sent the clipping to her airborne friend with a thank-you note. When Dale wrote back, he said that he planned to give Jo credit in the introduction of a new science book he was planning for very young children, with her parents' permission.

"You are a remarkable young lady," his letter concluded. "I'm sure I'll never meet anybody else five miles up in the clouds with her feet planted so firmly on the ground."

As usual, Jo had a scientific observation on the tip of her tongue. With a wrinkle of her nose and a shake of her head, she sighed, "That's impossible."

—*Nan B. Clark*

The Fourth Time
into the Water

I learned about courage in Spain, when I was nineteen.

I didn't mean to. I was supposed to be learning Spanish. I was there for a Spanish language intensive. It was a small, total immersion program with about eight students, taught by a native Spanish speaker. As soon as we met in Madrid, we were plunged in over our heads. Spanish was required; English forbidden.

The first thing I learned was how badly I spoke Spanish. An accent that had earned A's in high school was incomprehensible on the streets of Madrid. The first time I asked someone for directions, she stared at me, shrugged her shoulders, and walked away.

But speak Spanish morning to night and you get good at it. On the other hand, study Spanish culture morning to night and you get good and tired of it, at least if you're nineteen. We saw a cathedral every morning, a museum every afternoon. By week three, we were burned out. Another one-thousand-year-old castle? Ho hum.

That's why the trip organizers sent us to Cadiz. There's history there, too, of course. Cadiz was a Roman port, in use since blah blah blah. We didn't care. We were there for the beach. And Cadiz has a *great* beach. You got to it by driving a road that stretched into the ocean for miles, every inch of it lined with sand. We shrieked as we tumbled out of the bus to have fun.

We still learned things, of course. Play volleyball with Spaniards and you'll pick up Spanish phrases for "Out of bounds" and "Spike it!"

When somebody hit the ball over the heads of the back row and into the water, I learned something else. I learned about tides.

The ball skipped out across the top of the waves, always just out of reach of the laughing Spanish teenager chasing it. After a while, he gave up.

"I'll get it!" I called, running into the surf.

It took forever to catch up with the ball, which was racing out to sea, but I eventually did. When I turned around, I saw that I'd been carried a quarter mile from shore. More surprisingly, I saw that the current had carried me down the beach, past where the sand ended, to where there were only rocks. The waves boomed against them, sending spray high into the air.

I pushed the ball toward shore, and a wave threw it over my head. I gave up on the ball. I looked toward the beach. It was even further away. I got really scared, and I was sure I wasn't going to make it back.

But I did. I would swim and tread water and sometimes dive under to keep the biggest waves from pushing me back. When I got to the beach, I was exhausted, shivering from the cold of the deep water, and breathing in long, shuddering gasps. My new friends patted my shoulders, saying things like, "We're glad you made it back," and "See, that's why none of us chased the ball."

That was Wednesday. On Thursday, we went to the beach again. It was another perfect day. It was August and we were in Spain . . . ah. My friend Dan and I bodysurfed until we were exhausted and ready to get out of the water, which was good, because the weather was turning nasty.

When we got back to our towels, our teacher asked where the other students were. We pointed and laughed. Earlier I'd been warning (and teasing) the other students, all female, about the intense current. Now they were pretending that the current was running and that they were having trouble walking against it.

Except they weren't kidding. A stiff wind was blowing and it had intensified the outgoing tide. As we watched, the smaller girls got pulled farther out and one fell.

Our teacher wasn't that strong a swimmer, but he was a good-sized man. He, Dan, and I sprang into action. We waded out to the girls, getting stung by the rain the wind was whipping sideways. We each put an arm around two of the girls and led them back to safety. By the time we got to shore, the day was so gray that if you looked out over the water you couldn't tell where the sky ended and the sea began.

"Boy, am I glad you got us out of there," one girl said.

We were more than a little proud of ourselves. Then we heard it, shrill and far away.

"Ayudame!" Help me.

We looked across the waves. Two small heads bobbed just above the water, much farther out than the girls had been.

We called for a lifeguard, but our teacher explained this beach didn't have one. Dan and I looked at one another. We didn't want to go, but we knew we had to. We ran back into the surf. I don't know what Dan was thinking, but I was thinking about yesterday, when the current had taken me.

We got to the kids just as the waves dragged them under. I dove under the wave, where I was scoured by the racing sands, turned upside down, and slammed into one of the boys' legs. I grabbed hold. When I got done coughing the saltwater from my lungs, I saw that Dan had the other one.

We realized that, swimming against such a strong current, standard lifesaving holds wouldn't do. We'd all get pulled under. Dan and I came up with a new method. When a wave came crashing toward us, one that was sure to pull us under and farther out, we'd throw the kids into the air, forward, toward the beach. Dan and I would get pulled under, but the kids would keep breathing, and by the time we surfaced, they would be bobbing back to us.

It was clumsy and dangerous, but it worked. A throw at a time, one per overwhelming wave, we inched our way back to shallow water. We carried and then walked the kids back to land.

That was it! We'd done it! We were heroes! The coughing boys plopped down on the sand. Our teacher asked them where their parents were. They were crying, but one boy managed to answer. It wasn't what we wanted to hear.

"*Mi hermano.*"

"He's got a brother?" one of the girls asked.

Please God, let it be a language problem. Let us not have understood him. We just didn't have anything left.

As if on cue, we heard a voice cry out. We

turned. "Oh, crap."

If he hadn't been crying for help, we wouldn't have been able to see him. The sky had been gray earlier, now it was black. Everything was dark and wet, including the tiny face of the boys' little brother.

I glanced right. It was hard to tell through the rain, but it looked like he was already as far out as I'd been yesterday, when the current had swept me toward the rocks. There was no way that small child could handle that.

I glanced left. Dan was looking at me and trying not to look at me at the same time. When our eyes met, I said, "We have to, man."

Dan nodded, and we ran back into the waves. The retreating tide was so strong that the sand pulled away beneath our feet. We ran until we got into water deep enough to swim, then we dove in.

Dan was a faster swimmer. He reached the boy first and dove for him when the current sucked him under. Dan popped to the surface without him and dove again. This time, he came up with the kid and passed him over to me before disappearing as he got pulled under.

For several waves, I thought Dan was gone. I thought I was gone. I tried to stay on top of the water, but failed. I threw the kid toward the beach as a giant wave approached us.

"Nadar!" I yelled, which means, "to swim." Then

I went under, tumbling and choking. I remember thinking, *Great, I'm dying, and I'm trying to remember how to conjugate Spanish verbs.*

I swam hard. When I hit sand, I realized I was upside down. I turned and kicked for the sky. When I broke the surface, the top of the little kid's head slammed me in the chin. I couldn't hold him, but Dan was there to take him for a few strokes.

Slowly, incredibly slowly, we made it back to land. Our teacher met us in the shallows and took the little boy. Dan and I collapsed at water's edge.

We started laughing, just because we were alive. Eventually, we joined the others. The storm was starting to blow over, moving quickly, the way weather over water sometimes does, and here and there the sun was breaking through the clouds.

The boys were pretty much recovered. I wanted to turn them over to their parents, to make sure they were safe, but also (I was honest enough to know) to get what I felt was much-deserved gratitude for what we had done.

That didn't happen. The boys just wandered away, and Dan and I were left to make sense of what we'd done.

It's taken me some time, but I eventually made sense of that day on the beach in Spain, and it taught me about courage.

The first time I went into the water over my

head, it was out of ignorance and arrogance. I was nineteen, had never swum in the ocean, and thought I was indestructible.

The second time I went into the water, it was pride and duty. I wanted to make sure my friends were alright and to show the girls how strong I was.

The third time into the water, it was mostly social expectation. The girls were watching, and Dan was there. If he hadn't been there, hadn't met my eyes, I shudder to think what might have happened.

The fourth time into the water, that was courage, and it came from a very hard place. Dan and I were both so exhausted we could barely stand. We were bleeding from scraping our knees on the sand, and bruised and sore from hurling the boys back to life. And I at least knew exactly what I was risking. That poor little boy had been out as far as I'd been, when I'd thought I was going to drown.

But the biggest lesson about courage came when there were no congratulations. From somewhere, maybe the movies, I had this image in my head that now that I'd done something brave, it would be recognized. It would be recognized, and I would be transformed. I'd be a hero.

But no one said anything, and Dan and I were left to make sense of our actions by ourselves. And I eventually came to realize, slowly, in bits and pieces, that it was better that way. That leaving the act to stand on its own, without ceremony, left it pure. I didn't get a chance to rework my memory into some glowing thing, didn't have to retell it to an admiring crowd. I went on knowing precisely how scared I'd been, how small my courage had been, and how much I'd been driven by my own fears.

Since that time I've been in a number of crisis situations, and in all of them, what's anchored me has been that connection to the other person. I know how scared I am and how deeply I'm in over my head. But if I can cling to that connection running between me and the other person, I can act anyway, no matter how scared I am.

Finally, that day in Spain taught me that a courageous act is enough. It is all the reward I need. Because those little boys lived.

—*Greg Beatty*

It's the Little Stuff

"So, you're going to be okay?" Ray poked his head into the bathroom. He had on the Taylor Made, his favorite golf hat. It matched his shirt. He was sure to be made fun of at the club—the Designer Duds Dude.

"Yes. Go, already. Have fun." Cathleen was propped up naked against the sink, brushing her teeth.

"I could stay a while, in case you need some help."

"I'll be fine." The words slushed out in a mumble of foamy toothpaste.

"Well, if you're sure."

Cathleen spat into the sink. "I'm sure. Go. You deserve to get out."

Ray went over to Cathleen, gave her a peck on the cheek, and turned to leave. Cathleen waited for the click as the front door closed. Then the confidence slumped out of her shoulders. She raised an arm, wincing against the pain, and studied the bruises under her armpit, souvenirs from the crutches. She hopped over to the toilet and collapsed heavily down onto the seat.

The truth was she wasn't a bit sure she'd be okay. She surveyed the left foot, the one with a broken ankle encased in a heavy black boot, the one she was to put no pressure on, none whatsoever. She looked at the right one, the "good" foot, with the arch that crinkled in pain with every hop and the big toe joint inflamed with arthritis. She glanced at the five-inch ledge over which she must now, somehow, hop her body into the shower.

"The great thing about the boot," the doctor had said as he slid it over her foot, "is that you can remove it to take a shower." He had seemed very pleased with himself.

The house was quiet, so was the bathroom, except for a shy drip every so often from the faucet. Cathleen hadn't turned it off tightly enough. She looked over at the sink. It seemed so far away. She decided to let it drip. It wasn't worth the painful hops back over there.

"Well, I'm here." The words said aloud had a finality about them. What she meant was she was at that stage of life in which, if you got a headache, it could be a malignant brain tumor, and if you had diarrhea, it might be colorectal cancer, or if you broke your ankle, well, maybe it was the start of the rest of your life in a wheelchair. You know, when you're in your sixties.

Thinking of the wheelchair made her smile. Ray had been so excited when he came up with the idea of renting one. Truth was he didn't trust his wobbly wife on crutches and the walker took forever.

"Now we can get out and do stuff," he'd said. "You won't be so sore from hopping around."

It was a good idea. But Ray was a strong man, and his push sent the chair a long way. Cathleen chuckled as she remembered sticking her hands out in front, bracing for the impending crash as Ray bumped her along the parking lot toward the Olive Garden, and then the white alarm on the hostess's face as he wrenched her over the ledge at the doorway, nearly launching her headfirst into the restaurant. He'd underestimated how far the booted leg stuck out and managed to whack it on the sides of several doorways and chairs. Afterward in the parking lot, he forgot to set the brake while opening the car door and the chair rolled off, nearly tipping Cathleen over onto the grass alongside the pavement.

Her eyes got filmy with tears as she thought of Ray, and her face slid into a puffy softness. He'd been so attentive. Ray, the man who thought she had cleaned the house if she merely gathered up the throw rugs to toss them into the dryer. That man now vacuumed, washed dishes, took out the garbage, and fixed the pillows, just so, in the bed at night.

"I want you to keep that foot elevated," he would order.

Then he would leave a glass of water and the Vicodin on the nightstand, along with her eyeglasses and the novel she was reading for her book club. This is the same man who, from behind the newspaper, used to say, "While you're up, sweetie, could you get me a Coke?" Cathleen would get up, retrieve the soft drink, and place it and a treat-size Milky Way on the end table alongside his Lazy Boy. That man. Her heart felt mushy with love.

"You know," he had said, "this kind of thing is a jolt. What if something like this happened permanently to either of us? Maybe this is a dress rehearsal. Sure would change our lifestyle." The thought had made both of them scrunch up their faces in distaste and shake their heads, as if shaking away the terrifying thoughts. But the thoughts lingered. It could happen.

Now, here she was. Paralyzed by the thought of taking a shower. Such a little thing.

"Don't be a wimp!" Cathleen leaned over and began undoing the Velcro fasteners of the boot. She gently slipped her foot out of the boot, picked it up, and, stretching achy stomach and chest muscles—

who knew you used those muscles to hop about with crutches or a walker?—she propped the boot against the cupboard. There. Now it was ready for when she finished showering. She unwound the ace bandage, grimacing as she exposed the swollen foot, discolored green and yellowish blue.

What if she slipped on the wet shower floor? *I won't, I just won't,* Cathleen decided firmly. Gripping the sides of the walker, the raw, blistered heels of her hands screeching in pain, she lurched herself up off the toilet seat, reached around behind her, and slid open the glass shower door. It took a few more hopping turns until she could reach the shower nozzle and tilt it downward and toward the far side, away from the shower door. Then she turned on the water and slid the door closed.

She plopped back down on the toilet seat, panting. Sweat fell into the creases of her forehead. The unraveled ace bandage on the floor gave her an idea, and she reached over and began twining it around the good foot. Maybe that would cushion the pain for the big hop, the one that would land her into the shower.

Upright again, firmly gripping the arms of the walker, Cathleen slid open the other shower door. *Good,* she thought. *It worked.* The water was streaming down into the other end, and she would be able to land on a dry surface—if she could just get her body over that five-inch ledge.

Wobbling a bit as she balanced on the good foot, Cathleen lifted the walker into the shower and pulled it close up against the ledge. She closed her eyes tight against the image of her naked body crashing into the tile of the back wall, the foot breaking again as she fell. She muscled her arms into rigid supports, counted to three, and took a giant hop. The sides of the walker shook as she landed in the shower, and her heart pounded wildly.

She opened her eyes and stared in wonder. She was in the shower. She was okay. A crazy wild joy bubbled up inside, and she found herself laughing with glee. Cathleen closed the shower door behind her. "Damn, I'm good," she said. She maneuvered the walker around to face the gush of water at the other end of the shower. It would take several long hops and she was trembling, but she could do it.

The splash of warm water felt soothing over her body, washing away the sweat and dirt, massaging the sore shoulders and back, sweeping away some of the worry and tension. She watched the water swirl around the drain and disappear. It was going to be okay. They were going to be okay. Life was, after all, just a series of hops over all the little stuff.

—*Cathleen C. Robinson*

Valor Knows
No Stranger

Along the boulevards of bombed-out buildings, among the khaki-coated troops, the fire trucks, the red-crossed ambulances of death and near-death, sounded the familiar wail of approaching danger. The air-raid siren was not unexpected. This was war. This was London, 1941. For more than two years the population had absorbed a bludgeoning the likes of which had rarely been inflicted on a civilian population. The German aviators played their role, no better, no worse, just differently. They came to overtake and crush. A few English lives would not deter them in their quest to conquer the home of their mortal enemy. Scale sometimes blurs reason, and sometimes lack of scale reveals humanity. This is a story of humanity in its purest form.

A young Englishwoman pedaled her bicycle at a steady pace up the roadway. It was already past

6:00 P.M. and she wanted to get home to her two young children. She had brought them into this world of chaos as a result of her love for a young Canadian corporal. While he was off doing his war bit, the woman was holding up her end at home by working as a telegrapher during the day and as a mother and candle-burner at night.

With the first spit of the air-raid siren, Kathleen made a choice. Rather than stop to seek shelter, she would plunge on homeward in the hope that it was just a warning and not a full-blown air raid. She knew that the odds favored her slightly, and she just wanted to be home with her children at all costs. She pedaled harder as the siren sounded again, this time with much more urgency. Her bicycle slipped as she rounded the corner, just a half mile from her children, who by this time would be huddled under the stairway with their cousins and their aunt. The pavement seemed to jump up and bite her knee, opening it up to the sullen exposure of the early evening. Red blood spewed steadily from the scrape. Kit, as her friends knew her, took a punishing hold of the handlebars of her bike and returned its wheels to the pavement. She hurled herself and the bicycle forward with a sense of urgency. She hardly missed a second in the transition.

Everything moved at breakneck speed. Cars stopped and were left abandoned. Doors slammed.

Window shutters clamped shut with a sense of permanence. People walked at an accelerated pace. The fear and excitement were palpable as twilight descended.

Glancing up from her task, Kit saw the form of a woman just ahead on the edge of the roadway. She seemed to be struggling in a swaying stagger. *A drunk with no purpose and common sense.* As Kit let the judgment race through her brain she gained ground on the weaving woman wearing the long dark overcoat. She was pushing furiously at a baby stroller of which she had lost control in her panic. Kit was almost parallel to the fear-ridden woman and her child, and thinking of her own children, she was about to pass by quickly.

Suddenly everything went into slow motion. Over the building tops a black insect dotted the deepening sky. It grew larger quickly and then it began to spit darts of flame from its rigid wings. Kit's heart halted for a fraction of a second and then restarted with a motherly adrenaline surge. The German plane was beginning a strafing run over the end of the roadway, and it was headed quickly and lethally in her direction.

Kit jumped clear of her bike and landed, running in a protective crouch toward the nearest doorway. She got there only to find it firmly locked against the fear flying down their street. She turned, pressed her back to the door, and started to breathe sporadically.

The plane was growing larger and was giving off audible death notices. Kit could actually see the plumes of dirt and fire caused by the machine guns raking the street and houses. Eerie silence between gun bursts gave the impression that all the local people were simultaneously holding their breath.

The whole scene kept Kathleen plastered against the doorway. Slowly, or so it seemed, she turned her head to look back at the street in front of her and was horrified by the tableau playing out before her. The girl she had just passed had a firm grip on her baby's stroller's handle, hands pale, knuckles white. Her child screamed from the discomfort of the ride and the confusion of its mother. The girl stood motionless, eyes fixed and dilated, watching the plane bear down on her, frozen in the fear of an early death. Her mind, it seemed, had no order, no priority, no decision-making ability. Her mouth opened slightly, forming an unpronounced O. She and her child were about to become casualties of war.

The girl didn't feel the hand that grabbed her, nor did she see the hand that simultaneously grabbed the baby stroller from her frozen freeze of death and propelled them both toward the doorway. Not until her forehead smacked against the green-painted woodwork of the doorway did she break from her trance. She turned in confused panic, looking for her baby, in time to see Kathleen swiftly pushing the stroller with the terrified tot inside at her. Three humans huddled in haste.

The plane roared past, its guns spewing death and destruction on anyone and anything in its path. The threesome peeked from their poorly protected position. The quiet swept in behind the roar and swallowed them equally. Then, the roadway began to return to life, one heartbeat at a time. Doorways opened, curtains were pulled. Men and women peeked out at the death and destruction and were thankful to still be alive. The pace quickened, and a renewed energy punctuated the street scene. People began to help others. Damage was examined objectively. Vehicles were reoccupied. Hearts slowed to a regular beat.

Kit struggled to her feet. She was suddenly very tired. A quick visual check of her two doorway companions revealed smiles of survival. She assessed the scene in front of her, looking for her bicycle. It lay in a tangle at the side of the road where she had dropped it just moments before. She moved unsteadily toward it. Her legs gained strength as she remembered the reason for her ride. She quickly examined the bicycle and found it usable. She scrambled onto the seat and pushed herself off in the direction of her home. Suddenly, she was stopped. A thin white hand had grabbed the handlebar of her bicycle. It was the girl she had just saved from certain death, clutching her baby closely with her other arm.

"*Danke*," she said. "*Danke*."

Kit stared at the young German woman. The irony of the moment hung in the air between them. They both smiled weakly. The all-clear sounded, and Kathleen pedaled homeward, her heart bearing no animosity and, instead, filled with an understanding that only mothers share.

—David A. Walsh

When Traversing
Steep Terrain

I only knew Robin about eighteen months. We met in the fall of 1999 when we answered a mutual friend's invitation to take a pilgrimage to Scotland.

The six of us who signed on for the trip met one evening a month for the year preceding our departure. We discussed what we had been reading—*Crossing to Avalon, The Mists of Avalon, The Art of Pilgrimage*—and other books about the spiritual and practical aspects of travel. We plotted our nine-day itinerary, a triangle that took us from Glasgow, south to the Kilmartin Valley, west to Iona, north to Inverness, southeast to Lindisfarne, and then back home through Glasgow. We sorted out the logistics: budgets, flights, hotels, and car rental. We learned about our personal goals and what excited and scared us about making the journey.

A few months before we were scheduled to leave, Robin made an announcement: "I'm not sure I'm well enough to go."

I was dumbfounded. She had been so adamant about going with us. I thought no obstacle could keep her home.

"You will go on this trip," I declared, "even if we have to carry you."

The other women around the table didn't speak. I wasn't sure whether it was the bravery or stupidity of my statement that had silenced them. With the words spoken, however, we could no longer ignore what had always been a possibility.

Robin had breast cancer. After administering debilitating doses of radiation and chemotherapy, her oncologist had declared her in remission. But Robin had continued treatments with a Chinese herbalist and acupuncturist to rebuild her strength.

A week before we left for Glasgow, Robin took us through the Medicine Wheel, a decision-making tool founded on Native American traditions and ancient archetypes. Robin instructed us in the process, which involves posing a question and receiving responses from seven different "voices": Tradition, the Warrior, the Shaman, the Witch, the Tribal Chief, the Creator, and the Pattern Keeper. The eighth player, the Fool, begins the circuit by listening to the seeker's question and then flipping it into a seemingly unrelated query.

That transformed question goes to each character on the wheel for advice.

We each took turns asking a question about something we wanted to explore on the pilgrimage. The question I posed had to do with my life path: "Am I destined to use my creativity as a writer?" When I whispered this question to the Fool, she transformed it to, "Is the mountain high?" Traveling around the Wheel, I received responses ranging from, "They have been for centuries," from the Warrior, to the Pattern Keeper's nonchalant, "Mountains are what mountains are."

I was crushed. That was my answer? And what was all of this talk about mountains? I had left a corporate career, and for two years of "retirement," I had been searching for how I could make a difference in the world. I left the Medicine Wheel hoping that the riddle would unfold as I trekked the Highlands and the Lowlands.

With the help of a Chinese physician, Robin's characteristic willpower, and the confidence that she had five "sisters" willing to carry her bags, and her, if necessary, Robin was in the van when we headed to the Philadelphia airport on September 8, 2000. Twelve months of planning came alive when we landed in Glasgow the following morning. Each day brought new adventures and life lessons.

My most poignant moment occurred with Robin

on the highest point of Iona, a speck of land off the western coast of Scotland. We had all agreed to spend the day on our own. After practicing yoga on a hilltop overlooking the Abbey, I took a hike, heading toward a mountain I had seen in the distance. *I will make it that far and that high,* I kept thinking whenever a barbed wire fence blocked my way or a gust of Scottish wind enticed me back to the inn for a cup of tea. After hours of hiking across pastures, I arrived on the mountain peak. I was a mess: Shoes caked with sheep droppings, socks soaked through from wading across shallow streams, pants splattered with mud.

I sat at the top of the mountain, watching the sea brush the shores of the island. As I rose to leave, I spotted Robin. She stood on a rock several yards below me. Her face glowed as she looked out across Iona. A seasoned outdoorswoman, she had scaled much higher peaks around the world. Yet, this was one mountain she hadn't expected to climb. I sensed we were both celebrating.

My triumph was simple, but profound: allowing myself to get dirty, to wander alone, to be clumsy and even lost. She stood in wonder at the physical stamina she had mustered to reach the highest point on the island and the miracle of being alive.

When I caught up with Robin she was deciding which route to follow back to the village. She pointed to two paths: one to our left that looked like a straight, clear route to the bottom of the mountain, and another, more circuitous and rocky way to our right. After examining both of them, she, the experienced climber, chose the right-hand path.

"Sometimes the easier path is actually the more dangerous one," she said. I listened as she explained how even though the straight path looked easier, one misstep could lead to a hazardous fall down its steep, unprotected slope. The other, more crooked path might be slower and require more work, but it had a grassy shoulder alongside it to cushion a stumble.

As I absorbed Robin's hiking wisdom, I remembered my Medicine Wheel question and realized that Robin had given me my answer. I had psyched myself into believing that being a writer was a rocky path cluttered with solitude, criticism, and rejection. Though relinquishing my writing dream and going back to a safer, more established job might have seemed easier, I understood from experience the full meaning of Robin's climbing lesson. In reality, that so-called easy path had endangered my health, sapped my energy, and depleted my creative juices. I saw, too, that her guidance applied not only to my work, but also to my relationships and my spiritual path.

A few weeks after we returned home from Scotland, Robin was back in treatment for metastasized breast cancer. She continued her battle until her death on March 2, 2001.

I often visualize that mountaintop and hear Robin's words. What for her had been practical hiking advice has become a primer for how I approach life's daily challenges. Whenever I am tempted to run away, hide out, or relinquish a dream, I remember Robin's advice: Sometimes the easy route can be the more dangerous one. So, I keep climbing, following the woman who never just took the easy way.

—Linda M. Mastro

Mink Coat and Cherry Suite Dreams

I found her will in the filing cabinet, and in the silence of her big brick house I read these words:

> To my granddaughter Callie Ann I give my mink coat. . . . To my granddaughter Leslie Joan I give my cherry bedroom suite. . . .

The satin-smooth wood of the cherry dresser lay cool under my hand as I gazed out the window at fruit trees, bare-branched now in December, and wondered how such simple words could ever begin to tell the real story of the life they represented.

The night of January 18, 1918, was one of the coldest on record for that part of Kentucky. Bitter winter gripped the hills, and the snowfall was deeper than the tops of the fence posts. Like a bear in a rage, an arctic wind tried every crack in a little three-room house in the backwoods. Inside, a mother was giving birth, and she was weak. Dangerously weak. Ravaged by tuberculosis, she labored not just to bring her child into the world, but to hold on to life itself.

And so my granny was born. Tiny and cold, she squalled out her discomfort to any who would pity her. But working so hard to save the mother, the doctor had no time to save an infant. So she was wrapped, laid on the open oven door to keep warm, and fed butter and sugar in the corner of a rag.

She was brave, that baby, and somehow she survived—survived infancy, scarlet fever, and a head injury. Raised on squirrel and possum and dressed in made-over clothes or flour sack dresses, she possessed only one treasure: the determination to live. Season after season she followed her older brother through the woods to a one-room schoolhouse on Buck Creek—two and a half miles each way—often with no more breakfast than a piece of cornbread.

Growing up in the Great Depression, she dug May Apple roots and hoed tobacco for a little bit of cash. After borrowing her grandpa's mule to plow a garden spot in which to grow some food for winter, she told her grandma, "Give me a mule and fifty dollars, and I could make my way in the world."

She never got that mule or any real money, but her love of life carried her through marriage, motherhood, and a job in an aircraft plant during World War II. It took her out west to the dusty sagebrush country of Colorado and Utah, so different from the green rolling hills of Kentucky. Out west, she walked to a one-room schoolhouse once again—this time as the teacher.

Pretty things were few and far between in those postwar days; money hard-earned. "One day," she vowed. "One day I'll have a mink coat and a cherry bedroom suite." (She pronounced it "suit.")

From school teaching she went on to work for the soil conservation office. Through her thirties and forties and fifties, she drove the long road into town and labored, saving every penny she could put away. She saw her daughter marry, welcomed five grand-children into the world. Then daughter and family moved away, and there was nothing to keep her out west but thirty years of history.

So when her hometown of Leitchfield called her with an opening in the local soil conservation office, she answered and moved back to the emerald hills of Kentucky, myriad relatives, and countless memories. Back in the town of her growing-up years, she took a good look around. There sat the high school, which she dropped out of at seventeen to marry. There stood her parents' little house still perched on the hill by the creek, porch swing swaying in a lilac-scented breeze. She took all the savings she'd scraped together and bought a two-story brick house in a nice neighborhood.

Then in her sixties, she was still going strong. Years went by, and one exciting day she bought her cherry bedroom "suit." Her seventieth birthday came and went. She retired, and picked out the mink coat she'd dreamed about for so long.

Small—barely five feet tall—her fingers twisted with arthritis, she turned to quilting, tracing family genealogies, and planting fruit trees.

Eighty, eighty-two, eighty-four . . . her eyes as blue as ever, her smile as cheery and full of life. But her body began to betray her spirit. What could be wrong? Tired. She was so tired these days. But she forced herself to make the annual trip to Montana to visit daughter, grandchildren, and great-grandchildren, anyway, and took her first helicopter flight.

Back in Kentucky, the fall stretched long and warm and luscious. Her pear tree gave its fruit and her old-fashioned roses bloomed by the big brick house. But these days called for all the strength she could muster. Plans of trekking to overgrown cemeteries had to be shelved. Why was her leg swelling and food so hard to keep down?

Her weight dropped—110 pounds . . . 100 . . . 95. She spent more and more time in the cherry bed, surrounded by a lifetime of memories, her greatest need for courage now upon her. She was fighting for her life, and no one knew it. Every day a little weaker. Every day more pain.

"How are you doing, Granny?" I called to ask.

"Not so good, honey."

"I'll come."

She didn't try to talk me out of it, and that told more than a thousand words.

I came, but I found her surrounded not by her cherry bedroom suite, but by tubes, nurses, and hospital trappings. Found her fighting back against an unknown, ever-growing enemy and an ever-increasing pain. Yet, she still had that smile, those wide-open eyes, and the same zest for living that she'd shown in every season of her life, from the little baby on the open oven door to the elderly lady living all alone, planting fruit trees.

It was quick at the end. Quietly, a brave heart stopped beating, so quietly that most of the world never heard. But her fruit trees and flowers still bear faithful testimony. Her mink coat and cherry bedroom suite still speak of the invincible qualities she embodied. I close the door of the filing cabinet, running my hand once more over the deep, rich wood of the dresser. And I find comfort in knowing that who my granny was will live on long after her name is forgotten.

—*Leslie J. Wyatt*

Curtain Call

In the split second I balance in what I hope is a graceful *arabesque*, I fix my gaze on the figure in front of me. Its contours, after five years of shared ballet classes, are familiar. I know the tilt of the head, the turn of the hip joint, the angle of the rib cage. Yet, I don't know the woman. We've never talked.

Three times a week, midmorning, about ten women come to class. Are they women of leisure, or perhaps, like me, professionals who set time aside for an activity that is neither a workout nor a sport, nor defined as a hobby, and certainly, at this moment of burning muscles, feels nothing like art?

Ballet is a long, exacting, and frustrating journey. Unlike any other artistic pursuit—music, sculpting, painting, singing, writing, or even other forms of dance—there is no room for mediocrity. It demands the highest degree of perfection before one qualifies for a public performance. Thousands of hours of physical exertion yield a thimble-size progress. Not even my family will ever see me on stage.

My fellow dancers rarely speak. We share no locker-room bonding, even though we know one another's naked bodies. Breathless, I dash into the dressing room moments before class starts, clamp up my hair with a clip, shuck my street clothes, and pull on a black leotard and threadbare leg warmers with runs gaping at their sides. On my left, a woman puts on a ripped sweater with a scissored-off neckline. Another repairs her chaffed ballet slippers with electrical tape. The fad of gym clothes that spilled out of health clubs and into the streets passed over ballet studios. At the thresholds of these bastions of tradition, pretentiousness ends and humbleness begins. There is no faking it; this is no place for impostors. With no record of my life's achievements, I am only as good as my *pirouette*.

In class, watching the others, I scan for clues to the mystique of this lonely discipline in the faces and body language of my silent partners—the only audience I'll ever have.

Andrea always comes early to claim the top spot at the *barre*. It's a prime location with the only frontal mirror view when we move to the right as we dance. With a series of muted *ahems* and *harrumphs*, Andrea warns me not to intrude into her territory.

Connie's deep blue eyes crinkle at the sides when

she flashes me a delighted smile. Severe scoliosis must have threatened her with a hunched back, but her accurate and well-formed movements are of someone who had studied ballet seriously as a teenager. Who was this determined, smiling kid who fought the twisted cartilage and mutinous muscles, struggling with fate over her plans?

I love observing Elisa. Her young, pretty face is sprinkled with freckles; her voice is gentle; her hands are delicate; her head is tilted gracefully over an ample body. Yet, under the padded frame, the muscles are toned, for Elisa's *adagio* performance is seamless, light.

The snakelike scar of open-heart surgery peeking above the neckline of Claire's leotard is shiny and red against the wrinkled chest. In class, the seventy-year-old Claire beams, but her smiles are out of context. So are her movements. She follows us, not the music. When the teacher addresses her, Claire reads her lips, nods, but she does not hear. She feels the music through its vibration.

Bea does not ask questions. Rather, she informs the teacher how others have instructed her in years past. She comments on the speed of the music, on its adaptability to a particular combination, and on the state of the wooden floor with regards to the day's humidity. She shakes her head in disgust as her knees and elbows fail to coordinate with her body when it is propelled into the air. It's the wrong music.

It's the wrong floor. It's the wrong weather. Pouting, she retreats to the resin box.

Oh, that resin, which I hate, but which Carol can't get enough of. Instead of scrunching the bottom of her slippers in the box to apply a film needed for friction with the polished floor, Carol sneaks a glance at the open door. When she does not see the studio owner who forbids it, she scoops a handful of the yellowish stuff and sprinkles it on the floor at each of the spots she plans to occupy.

It is my turn to cover the floor in three giant leaps. I psyche myself. I'm a gazelle. This is the moment years of training come together. I cut the air on planes few people ever dare to move through. My muscles taut, I reach high. My right leg is stretched forward toward my destination, the left pulls hard toward the opposite corner. In the split second I hold at the top of my jump, I check the placement of my fingers, my abdomen, my shoulder blades. Invisible strings control all of me from within.

I am a soaring swan.

But the awkward figure in the mirror, wearing my outfit and bearing my face, looks neither like a swan nor a gazelle.

So what? I am ready to show off with a series of jumps. My muscles burning with exertion, I land into my most graceful *pirouette*. Damn. The resin. I can't turn in it.

A vision of my leaping figure in the mirror flashes

through me. I am suddenly depressed. I mumble about my aching back and slink out.

I dash down the stairs to the basement. I begin to pull off my leotard—and stop short. In the dressing room, among a cluster of four-year-olds in varying stages of undress, two men are helping their daughters put on hot pink tutus.

"Excuse me," I stammer, and hastily stretch the fabric over my exposed breast.

One man swallows hard. The other sheepishly extricates his daughter and gets up to leave.

"It's okay," I say. Some things have changed in the world of ballet after all: Fathers take interest. "I'll shower at home." I grab my raincoat.

From the studio, the final notes of "reverence"— bowing to our teacher and our imagined audience— cascade off the mirrors. My imagined audience is throwing tomatoes at me. At the exit door, I leave my coat, turn, and rejoin the group in a final bow.

What am I doing here? Ballet class is the only place where I am a wimp. A place where I back away from Andrea's territory, from Carol's resin, where I relinquish the dressing room to men.

Yet, with the final melodious notes, as a pleasant ache spreads through my legs, I relish it all. The day after tomorrow, I'll come back for more.

—Talia Carner

Hope Where You Least Expect It

I was relieved and grateful that my younger son, Eric, was not old enough to be drafted during the Vietnam War. I thought I had escaped that kind of parental stress and loss until a few years later, when I stood by his hospital bed.

A young drunk driver had lost control of his truck and struck Eric as he stood on the sidewalk in front of a shop where he worked after school and weekends in a nearby small town. The town's main street was gravel and blacktop, and Eric had been dragged off the sidewalk for more than a hundred yards. For more than a week his older brother and I had kept a bedside vigil at the hospital, as Eric, swathed in bandages and casts, fought for his life.

Injuries to his face and head would eventually heal, but he would need plastic surgery a dozen times over the next five years. During extensive surgery the night after the accident, a six-inch pin was inserted into Eric's shattered elbow, and that arm had lost most of its mobility. The surgeons predicted he would have a permanent limp as well.

While I was grateful that Eric had survived the accident, I was heartsick over his injuries and angry that life had dealt him such an unfair blow at an early age. As I looked down at my tall, bright, and kind son, it seemed a cruel act of fate.

Eric was sedated for pain much of the time, but when he was able to talk with us, he made it clear that he did not want his girlfriend to see him. Because of the facial scars he knew he would have and the impairments he faced, he thought his days of dating were over—before he'd even reached his twentieth birthday.

Friends who came to visit Eric at the hospital later that terrible week talked me into going out with them for a hot meal. I was reluctant, but Eric insisted I go.

Over dinner, my already low mood was abraded further by a group of young people at the next table: three good-looking young men and their dates. Collegiate types, they seemed to me, out for a night of fun. Not a care in the world.

They laughed with each other and kidded their waiter, a little too loudly to suit me in my gloom. The girls giggled. They were all in a celebratory mood. I definitely was not, although my companions did their best to cheer me up.

One of the young men in that nearby group was particularly striking. A Viking type, he looked to me, with fine blond hair, brilliant blue eyes, and wide, muscled shoulders. He reminded me a little of Eric as he had been before the accident.

This handsome man looked to be in his early twenties. I would have guessed him to be a college football player. From what I could see above table level, he certainly had the build for football. When I glanced that way, he was holding hands with the loveliest of the three girls at the table. From time to time, they leaned toward one another to touch shoulders.

Picking at my food, I tried to be polite and concentrate on my friends' conversation. But my mind kept returning to my son in his hospital bed, facing a difficult future. My child, who should have been out on a date like the young people nearby.

The small dance band that had played soft music during dinner suddenly launched into a raucous version of "The Marine's Hymn" as a waiter carried in a cake with flaming candles and placed it before the young man who reminded me of Eric. Then his friends sang "Happy Birthday" to him and cheered as he blew out the candles. The pretty girl leaned over and kissed him.

After the cake was served, one of the couples left the table to dance. I overheard the "birthday boy" ask his date, "Shall we?"

I looked their way again, expecting to see at least a six-foot frame of youth stand up. Instead, I saw two strong hands push back from the table and turn himself in a wheelchair I had not been able to see before. The Viking extended a hand to the girl who had kissed him and pulled her onto his lap. With her arms around his neck, he gave a powerful shove to the chair's wheels and they zipped out onto the dance floor, where he maneuvered the chair expertly in time to the music.

And I saw he had no legs below the knees. His face, though, glowed with happiness as they danced.

My eyes filled with tears. I excused myself and rushed to the powder room before my friends could see me crying.

When I returned to the hospital the next morning, Eric was awake and I told him about that courageous ex-Marine and his girl who was obviously proud of him. My son lay quietly for a while. Then he asked if I would go out to get him some magazines.

As I walked out of the room, I looked back and saw him reach with his good hand for the bedside telephone. For the first time, he asked the hospital switchboard operator to dial his girlfriend's number. Suddenly, the room seemed brighter and Eric's future not so frightening. Fate, which can be cruel, can also surprise us with unexpected gifts of courage.

—*Marcia E. Brown*

Home Is Where
the Hearth Is

There is an old Gaelic expression that states, "May the roof above you and the hearth before you always be your own." Reflecting upon the history of war-torn, famished Ireland, it is not difficult to understand why a safe haven, a home, has been so highly regarded by the Irish.

Such were my thoughts as I surveyed the brownstone on West 18th Street, bordering New York City's Greenwich Village. The day was cold, gray, and dreary as I stood outside the wrought iron gate surrounding the home. At the turn of the century, this modest building meant the world to Maggie O'Connor, an immigrant from County Clare. One of my biggest regrets was that I'd never had the opportunity to meet dear Maggie, who was my great-grandmother.

Bursting with optimism, eighteen-year-old Maggie landed at Ellis Island in 1892 with little more than five dollars in her pocket and the clothes on her back. But she wasted no time lamenting what little she had and secured a position that afternoon as a cook's helper in a wealthy Park Avenue household.

A year later she married a fellow Irisher, a handsome longshoreman from Donegal. The two set up housekeeping on the third floor of the brownstone that now stood before me. Seven years and five babies later, he was killed, tragically, crushed between the dock and some itinerant cargo.

How often I have wondered what thoughts must have gone through her mind at that time. Did she consider returning to Ireland? Putting her children up for adoption? Turning to her mainstay, the Catholic Church? I like to imagine her squaring her narrow shoulders, jutting her chin forward, and swallowing her fears. Women in my family have always been a pillar of strength, and I like to attribute that trait to Maggie.

My grandmother remembered little about her father. What was very clear to her, however, was that shortly after his death, the family moved "downstairs." In hindsight, it seems that without her husband's income, Maggie could no longer afford the upstairs apartment, and she lost no time in relocating her young family to the basement quarters. Once situated, she convinced the owner of the brownstone to accept a bartered arrangement. Every morning, she would fill each open heating grate of the twelve units above with coal and then prepare breakfast and later prepare dinner for all of the boarders. In exchange, she and her children could live in the basement quarters rent-free.

The owner must have agreed, as my grandmother recalls Maggie herding the five children into that "downstairs" apartment. But my grandmother's memories were not depressing. Rather than "dark and damp," as one might expect, my grandmother described their home as being "light and bright." And she said that every day brought a new adventure.

But if Maggie had painted a rosy picture for her children, in reality her life was one of continuous work and little leisure. Every morning she carried buckets of coal to the twelve families living upstairs. Then, while keeping an eye on her own brood, she would prepare breakfast for the boarders, serving them in the large dining area. Her own children would then eat in the kitchen, and my grandmother recalled that leftovers had never tasted so delicious.

Several hours each afternoon, Maggie worked as a laundress, and the children accompanied her to various homes along "the Avenue" (Seventh). During the late afternoon, they returned to the boarding house to prepare dinner. As time was a commodity not to be squandered, she filled the evening hours by taking in "piecework," sewing by the fire.

If times seemed hard, she never complained. There was food on their table and a roof over their heads. In Ireland, she had had neither, for famine and poverty were everywhere.

So many times in my life I have thought about Maggie, my great-grandmother, and how hard she worked. It was through her back-breaking labor that my grandmother was able to learn a trade, that my mother was able to attend college, and that I was able to obtain a graduate degree. Because of her sacrifices, I have inherited a life of more ease and luxury.

Over the years when enjoying a relaxing weekend, I have often wished I could have spent part of it with Maggie. Perhaps we could have enjoyed tea and scones at a five-star hotel, indulged in a manicure and massage at an exclusive spa, or taken in a movie or a play at an upscale theater. But somehow, I know she would not have enjoyed these experiences; she would have been nervous, frightened, and perhaps even suspicious of such pampering and leisure activity. I can almost imagine her politely declining my invitations and escaping to the safety of her basement apartment, her familiar mending nestled in her lap.

So deep were my thoughts as I stared at the brownstone, that I did not notice that the drizzle had become a downpour. As I struggled with my umbrella, the present owner opened the door. He seemed to be of a gentle nature, and smiled shyly and asked if he could assist me.

"Oh, I'm sorry," I stammered. "I was just admiring your home. Someone I knew used to live here a very long time ago."

He brightened visibly and asked if I would like to take a look inside. He seemed to be quite proud of the brownstone.

"I'd love to," I responded, climbing the porch steps.

As I walked through the large foyer, dining room, and parlor, I could appreciate his pride. The home was magnificent and had been restored to its Victorian splendor. But my interest was not on the main floor.

"Would I be able to see the basement?" I asked.

The owner smiled. "The basement? Now, that's an unusual request. How did you know that is my favorite part of the house?"

The stairs were located behind the kitchen, and as I descended, I thought of dear Maggie hauling endless buckets of coal up those very same steps.

Reaching the bottom, I gasped. Despite the gray afternoon and the rain beating against the high basement windows, the entire area seemed to be bathed in light. With overstuffed chairs and ottomans surrounding an open hearth, the room felt like a homey refuge. But there was more. An inexplicable benevolent force seemed to permeate the room—as if it were almost a holy place, a place that housed only love.

On the mantel was a Greek statue, and I inquired about it.

"It's Hestia, the goddess of home and hearth," the owner answered. "She watches over this house. While I love what she represents, I am not fond of the name 'Hestia.' It seems a bit too formal, a bit cold, doesn't it?"

"Have you ever considered calling her Maggie?" I asked him. And suddenly, rays of sunlight streamed through the basement windows.

—Barbara Davey

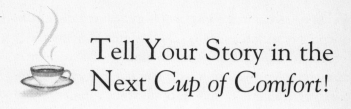

Tell Your Story in the Next *Cup of Comfort*!

We hope you have enjoyed *A Cup of Comfort for Courage* and that you will share it with all the special people in your life.

You won't want to miss our next heartwarming volumes, *A Cup of Comfort for Sisters* and *A Cup of Comfort Devotional*. Look for these new books in your favorite bookstores soon!

We're brewing up lots of other *Cup of Comfort* books, each filled to the brim with true stories that will touch your heart and soothe your soul. The inspiring tales included in these collections are written by everyday men and women, and we would love to include one of your stories in an upcoming edition of *A Cup of Comfort*.

Do you have a powerful story about an experience that dramatically changed or enhanced your life? A compelling story that can stir our emotions, make us think, and bring us hope? An inspiring story that reveals lessons of humility within a vividly told tale? Tell us your story!

Each *Cup of Comfort* contributor will receive a monetary fee, author credit, and a complimentary copy of the book. Just e-mail your submission of 1,000 to 2,000 words (one story per e-mail; no attachments, please) to:

cupofcomfort@adamsmedia.com

Or, if e-mail is unavailable to you, send it to:

A Cup of Comfort
Adams Media
57 Littlefield Street
Avon, MA 02322

You can submit as many stories as you'd like, for whichever volumes you'd like. Make sure to include your name, address, and other contact information and indicate for which volume you'd like your story to be considered. We also welcome your suggestions or stories for new *Cup of Comfort* themes.

For more information, please visit our Web site: *www.cupofcomfort.com.*

We look forward to sharing many more soothing *Cups of Comfort* with you!

Contributors

Beth Rothstein Ambler ("Eva: Princess of True Grit") resides in New Jersey with her husband, Chuck, and her two canine companions. She enjoys writing short stories and inspirational articles for *Real Living with MS* and *Inside MS* magazines. This is her third contribution to the *A Cup of Comfort* collection.

Greg Beatty ("The Fourth Time into the Water") has held an assortment of odd jobs, including massage therapist and bartender on a charter boat. He supports his writing habit by teaching for the University of Phoenix Online. When he's not at his computer, he enjoys cooking, practicing martial arts, and having complex interpersonal relationships.

Maura Bedloe ("Something More") writes from her seaside home in a small village in southeastern Tasmania, Australia, where she lives with her husband and two small children. Her work has been published within Australia, the United Kingdom, and the United States. Through her storytelling, she seeks to unearth and bring to light the wonderful and miraculous tales that lie buried in the lives of ordinary human beings.

Sande Boritz Berger ("Ninety-Day Wonder") lives in Manhattan and Bridgehampton, New York, with her husband and has two daughters. After nearly two decades as a script writer and video/film producer, she returned to her first passion, writing fiction and nonfiction. Her award-winning short stories, poetry, and essays have been published in numerous anthologies and literary journals.

Amy Brady ("The Shtick of a Lifetime") currently lives in Kansas City, Missouri, where she works for a marketing firm. She holds a bachelor's degree in creative writing from the University of Kansas. In her spare time she works as a freelance writer and improvisation comedian.

Mary Brockway ("Live") has been writing steadily for thirty years. She has published short stories and articles in various anthologies and periodicals, and has written several books, one of which won second place in the 2002 Pacific Northwest Writers Association literary contest. The mother of five and grandmother of eight shares a home in Seattle, Washington, with her husband of many years.

Marcia E. Brown ("Hope Where You Least Expect It") is an Austin, Texas, senior citizen whose writing has appeared in magazines, newspapers, and anthologies. Specializing in humor, she has completed a book of her funniest family stories. Marcia is a member of the National League of American Pen Women and the Texas Writers' League.

Danya-Zee Bulkin ("Against All Odds on the Field of Dreams") lives in Johannesburg, South Africa, where she is a content editor/consultant involved in marketing services and a freelance writer. She feels optimistic about South Africa's future but is saddened that it is often portrayed as a country in despair, and so she writes stories that reflect the hope and promise of her "beautiful nation" for all the world to read.

Christy A. Caballero ("Of Silk and Steel" and "Leaning into the Harness") is a freelance writer and photographer who lives a couple of deer trails off the beaten track in Oregon. The woods, the sound of the river, or the sight of the ocean can all put a smile on her face. Her work has earned national awards, including the National Federation of Press Women Communications Contest and the Dog Writer's Association of America "Maxwell" Award. Christy has contributed stories to other volumes of the *A Cup of Comfort* series.

Talia Carner ("Curtain Call"), of New York, is a former business consultant to *Fortune* 500 companies and the former publisher of *Savvy Woman* magazine. Since becoming a full-time writer, she has published more than thirty award-winning personal essays and short stories and written three novels. Her first novel, *Puppet Child*, has been lauded by more than forty independent book reviewers; her second novel, *China Doll*, will be published in 2004.

Candace Carrabus ("Love's Imprint") is a Web site designer who lives on a farm with her husband and daughter outside St. Louis, Missouri. They have eight cats, a dog, and yes, a couple of horses. She still enjoys riding, but never forces her mounts into the water.

Cinda Williams Chima ("The Art of Living") changed college majors fifteen times, exiting with a degree in philosophy. Today, she is a dietitian with MetroHealth Systems in Cleveland and a freelance writer specializing in health and family issues. Married and the mother of two sons, Chima lives in Strongsville, Ohio.

Nan B. Clark ("Steady as She Rises") lives in Beverly, Massachusetts, with her husband, Tom, whom she met when they were both rookie newspaper reporters. A special needs tutor, she knows how courageous children can be.

Dan Cooper ("The Courage of John Bankston") is a freelance writer/editor living in the Texas Hill Country. He has been a sports and news editor, and currently edits a newsletter column for the Writers' League of Texas. He wrote a book introduction for the Barnes & Noble Digital Library and is working on his first novel.

Barbara Davey ("Home Is Where the Hearth Is") is a health care administrator at a major teaching hospital by day. After hours, she celebrates her Celtic heritage with storytelling, paying homage to those ancient souls who were "walkers-between-the-worlds." Nearly a dozen of her inspirational essays have been published in literary magazines and anthologies. She and her husband, Reinhold Becker, live in Verona, New Jersey.

Kirsten and Lise Day ("Darkness and Sunshine"), mother and daughter, both live on the beautiful east coast of South Africa known as the Garden Route. Kirsten is an environmental scientist in Cape Town. She has maintained a close friendship with her hiking companion, Sue, in North Carolina. Lise lectures in English communication at the local Technikon. She also enjoys quilting, painting, writing, and gardening.

Danielle deLeon ("You Got Beat by a Girl"), a former Zamboni driver and bitter secretary, is a freelance writer living in Belmont, California. Her passions include ice hockey goaltending, writing, and keeping her ornery parrot in line.

Susan DeMersseman, Ph.D. ("The Green Chalk Heart"), lives in the San Francisco Bay Area with her husband and two teenagers. A psychologist, she works in schools, conducts parent and teacher workshops, and consults on media projects for children. Susan has written for national and local publications, and has just completed a collection of essays.

Betty Downs ("Angel of Courage") is the mother of four grown sons and has been a homemaker most of her life. She has lived in Montana, North Dakota, South Dakota, and Wyoming. Now widowed, she lives in Black Hawk,

South Dakota, and enjoys writing, gardening, traveling, and watching her seven grandchildren grow.

John Gaudet ("Dad's Belt") lives in Prince Albert, Saskatchewan, Canada. A freelance writer whose articles and essays have been published in several print and online publications, he is presently working on a novel. He enjoys reading, writing, and spending time with his wife, Chantalle, and their daughter, Charisa.

Tanya Ward Goodman ("Moving Grandma West") is a freelance writer and full-time mother. She lives in Los Angeles, California, with her husband, David, and son, Theodore Roscoe. She is currently working on a memoir chronicling her experience with her father and his Alzheimer's disease.

Christina Hamlett ("The Promise of Indiana"), a former actress and director, works as a script coverage consultant. Her writing credits include seventeen books, over a hundred plays and musicals, two optioned screenplays, multiple short films, and several hundred magazine articles and interviews. She and her husband, Mark, reside in Pasadena, California.

Linda Henson ("I Thought I Could Fly") has been published in various anthologies and newsletters, and is a contributor to the local newspaper. She formerly taught in public schools and presently teaches in a Bible College in the Bahamas, where she now resides.

Loretta Kemsley ("Wildfire"), of Sylmar, California, first sat in a saddle at six months. Her childhood companions included Champion, Trigger, Koko, and Mr. Ed. At age eight, Gene Autry hired her to do stunt riding in *The Buffalo Bill Jr.* television series. Training horses came natural as a career. Her memories of Mr. Ed were featured in *The Encyclopedia of TV Pets*.

Caroline Kennedy ("What If?") has been a traveler and a writer most of her adult life. During the past decade, she has worked for a charity in Bosnia, Croatia, and Azerbaijan, helping refugees with physical disabilities. Currently, she is setting up a retreat and creative study center in Costa Rica, and writing her second book. Her home base is London, England.

Beate Korchak ("The Eagle and the Sparrow") resides in Brantford, Ontario, Canada with her husband, Terry, and nine-year-old daughter, Whitney. She enjoys writing and feels fortunate to be at that stage in life where she has the opportunity to follow those dreams.

Emmarie Lehnick ("The Power of Words"), of Amarillo, Texas, is a retired teacher with a B.S. and M.A. in English/Speech. She is an award-winning Toastmaster and a member of Inspirational Writers Alive. She and her husband have a daughter, son, and four grandboys.

Janet Lindstrom ("Reinventing Myself") is the pseudonym of a high school English teacher who lives in a rural paradise in the Midwest. Her passions include teaching, writing, gardening, travel, her children, and her wonderful husband.

Ruby Long ("Encounter in Yucatan") is a new writer who pens tales about her life in Oakland, California, her travels, and other places she has called home.

Linda M. Mastro ("When Traversing Steep Terrain") lives in Neavitt, a small waterfront village on Maryland's Chesapeake Bay, with her husband and yellow Lab. A freelance writer, she is committed to telling stories that promote physical health, personal growth, and spiritual awareness. An avid yogi, she studies and teaches in the Kripalu tradition.

Patricia A. Murphy ("Mercy from the Flames") was an award-winning fiction writer and widely published nonfiction writer specializing in health, environmental, and lifestyle issues. She is the author of *Treating Epilepsy Naturally: A Guide to Alternative and Adjunct Therapies* (Contemporary Books, McGraw Hill) and was editor/publisher of the *Epilepsy Wellness Newsletter*. A few months after writing this story, Patricia lost her life to an epileptic seizure. A native New Yorker, she made her home in the Pacific Northwest with her partner of fifteen years, Michael DiBitetto, an artist.

Carol Padgett, Ph.D. ("Counter Actions"), works as a health ministry consultant in Birmingham, Alabama. She co-developed the nationally acclaimed Balm of Gilead end-of-life program. Author of the *Keeping Hearth & Home* series, she hosts a nineteenth-century news program on National Public Radio and offers period tips in the first video history of the Farmers' Almanacs.

Joy Pincus ("No More Waiting") lives in central Israel. A contributing writer to the *Jerusalem Post* and *Women's E News*, she is also the administrative director of the Global Research in International Affairs (GLORIA) Center and the assistant editor for the *MERIA Journal*. Another of her stories appears in *A Cup of Comfort for Friends*.

Kathryn Presley, Ph.D. ("The Rose of Tucumcari"), recently celebrated her fiftieth wedding anniversary with her husband, Roy. They enjoy frequent visits with their son, daughter, and four grandchildren. A retired English professor, she is now a freelance writer with more than forty published stories in magazines, professional journals, and anthologies, including other books in the *A Cup of Comfort* series. She also enjoys speaking to women's groups and reading.

Kimberly Ripley ("A Year in the Life of a Heroine") lives in Portsmouth, New Hampshire, with her husband, five children, and faithful dog, Philly. She is a full-time freelance writer and published author of five books, including several volumes of *A Cup of Comfort*. Her Freelancing Later in Life workshop has traveled to several states and her book by the same title has received numerous awards.

Cathleen C. Robinson ("It's the Little Stuff") recently retired after thirty-six years of teaching Spanish and courses in the humanities at a boarding school in New England. Since then, she has directed her energies toward creative writing, her perennial flower beds, pampering her grandson, and cheering the Revolution soccer team alongside her husband of twenty-five years. She does miss teenagers, though, and in her stories frequently invents new ones to worry about.

Marie Schnerch ("You've Got to Be Kidding") lives in Winnipeg, Canada, where she has been writing for about five years. Her articles, essays, and creative nonfiction stories have been published in newspapers and magazines.

Libby Simon, M.S.W., R.S.W. ("Where Doves Dare to Fly"), is a retired child welfare and school social worker who has worked in the public education system in Canada. Now a freelance writer, she focuses on social/educational issues affecting children. Her book *Don't Fight, It's Not Right*, available online through the Manitoba Text Book Bureau, features a violence prevention program for kindergarten to grade three.

Lisa J. Solomon ("This View") is a freelance writer based in Los Angeles. She specializes in food writing, and her essays and articles have appeared in the *Atlanta Journal-Constitution, Vegetarian Times, Walking Magazine, The Canadian Jewish News*, and other publications. She is a finalist in the Soul Making Literary Prize, the Writer's International Forum, and the Maui Writers Conference Screenwriting

Competition. When she isn't cooking up new food stories, she is polishing the second draft of her first novel.

Lu Stitt ("Go, Lu, Go!") lives in Cottonwood, Arizona, where she writes and is the editor of the *Cottonwood Journal Extra*. She loves to turn words into entertaining and informative stories and to play outdoors. She lives by the philosophy that no goal is too tough to try.

Lois Greene Stone ("Keys Made of Ivory") is a poet and author whose works have been syndicated worldwide. Collections of her personal items, photographs, and memorabilia are in major museums, including twelve different divisions of the Smithsonian. She lives in upstate New York.

Annemarieke Tazelaar ("Westward, How?") moved from The Netherlands to the United States with her family after World War II and has spent most of her adult life in Washington state, teaching children of all ages. Presently, she owns and manages a business in Seattle. Her stories appear in other volumes in the *A Cup of Comfort* collection.

Peggy Vincent ("All Creatures Great and Small") is the author of *Baby Catcher: Chronicles of a Modern Midwife* (Scribner 2002), a memoir of her years as a home birth midwife. Peggy's writing has appeared in *Reader's Digest, The Christian Science Monitor, Skirt!*, and various other publications, including *A Cup of Comfort*. She lives in Oakland, California, with her husband and teenage son, and two adult children live nearby.

Gillian Wakelin ("The Ultimate Power Pole") lives near Auckland, New Zealand, on twenty-three green rolling acres. A husband, four sons, four daughters-in-law, four grandchildren, and a menagerie of geriatric animals are her family. She is belatedly studying for a bachelor of arts in English and is also determinedly pursuing her life-long ambition to write full-time.

David A. Walsh ("Valor Knows No Stranger"), born during World War II, grew up in Canada. The father of four, he spent most of his professional life as a high school educator. He lives with his wife, Donna, in retirement in St. Andrews, New Brunswick, Canada.

Leslie J. Wyatt ("Mink Coat and Cherry Suite Dreams") is a homeschooling mom and freelance writer. She and her husband have been blessed with six children and live in Missouri on a "sort of" farm with chickens, a garden, a dog, cats, and a fair share of mice.

Lorraine Wylie ("Let's Keep Dancing"), of Northern Ireland, has been married for twenty-six years to her husband, Michael. They recently bought a small farm in France, and have three children and a new daughter-in-law. Her family is the source of her inspiration, both in her writing and in living with epilepsy.

About the Editor

Colleen Sell has long believed in the power of story to connect us with our inner spirits, the Higher Spirit, and one another. Her passion for storytelling has been inspired and nurtured by many mentors, a gift she is paying forward by helping others to share their stories.

The editor of more than sixty published books, Colleen has also authored and ghostwritten several books. She is the former editor-in-chief of *Biblio* and *Mercator's World* magazines, and has been a journalist, columnist, essayist, and copywriter.

She lives with her husband, T. N. Trudeau, in a nineteenth-century Victorian on a forty-acre lavender and tree farm in the Pacific Northwest, where she continues to write tales both tall and true.

Also Available in the . . .

Each *Cup of Comfort* book features over 50 exceptional stories of ordinary people who have overcome great obstacles, persevered through thick and through thin, and found the power to control their own destinies. Readers will laugh and cry out loud as they share in the many moving experiences detailed within these pages.

ISBN: 1-58062-524-X
Trade Paperback, $9.95

ISBN: 1-58062-622-X
Trade Paperback, $9.95

ISBN: 1-58062-844-3
Trade Paperback, $9.95

The recipes include: